Problems in American Civilization

The CHALLENGE
of The CITY
1860–1910

EDITED WITH AN INTRODUCTION BY

Lyle W. Dorsett

UNIVERSITY OF MISSOURI – ST. LOUIS

D. C. HEATH AND COMPANY · Lexington
A division of RAYTHEON EDUCATION COMPANY

Library of Congress Catalog Card Number: 68-8292

INTRODUCTION

IN 1880 the Bureau of the Census published two volumes of documents entitled *Social Statistics of Cities*. This act marked the beginning of the federal government's interest in urbanization. Federal recognition of the city symbolized the whole nation's growing awareness of the significance of urbanization. Indeed, throughout the period from the Civil War to World War I a host of Americans from many walks of life began talking and writing about the city. Why was there so much interest in the city after the Civil War? After all, cities had developed rapidly before 1865. One answer is that by the mid-nineteenth century the character of urbanization had changed. The industrial revolution had come to the United States, bringing a marked acceleration of urban expansion. Only nine cities had populations numbering 100,000 or more in 1860, but by 1900 there were thirty-eight cities with over 100,000 inhabitants, and during the next twenty years the figure increased to sixty-eight. Industries demanded thousands of new workers, and the prospect of high wages drew many Americans to the cities from farms and small towns. Countless farms were deserted, and some small communities actually disappeared from the map. At the same time the quest for a better life lured thousands of European immigrants to the industrial cities. European immigration to the United States greatly increased after the Civil War, reaching 5,200,000 in the 1880's — the peak for the century. Although immigration declined slightly during the 1890's because of the depression, it surged to over 8,200,000 in the first ten years of the twentieth century.

The industrial revolution caused problems unprecedented in American history. It is true that the city fulfilled the promise of American life for some people. Real wages increased in several industries, and a wide variety of white-collar jobs were created to meet the needs of industry and the city. For many others, however, the industrial city offered poverty and despair. Labor markets became glutted in some industries. Unemployment and lower wages ensued. In most cities the demand for housing outstripped the supply, forcing the lower income classes into old buildings hastily converted into tenements. Inadequate transportation facilities kept workers and their families in slum dwellings near their places of employment. And very soon sewer systems were overtaxed when many families moved into buildings that once had been warehouses or dwellings for only one or two families. Consequently, filth collected and disease spread. To complicate matters even more, police and fire departments were as inadequate as the sewer systems, thus adding fire and crime to the growing list of urban problems.

Rapid industrialization and urbanization combined to create serious problems of municipal government, and there were no precedents to follow in solving them. As a result, political bosses emerged to fill part of the power vacuum that existed in the cities. Men such as William Marcy "Boss" Tweed in New York, Abraham Ruef in San Francisco, and Philadelphia's Vare brothers took advantage of the situation in order to gain political power. They offered jobs, food, fuel and clothing to the new immigrants and the destitute poor — in return for their votes on election day. Once in control of the city government the bosses would line their own pockets with the taxpayers' money by letting contracts to businessmen who were willing to pay a "lug" to the machine, or granting a streetcar franchise to the corporation that was willing to pay the highest fee to the bosses.

Widespread graft and corruption, plus the blight of poverty, slums, disease and vice, could not be ignored long. Indeed, these problems had grown so severe that some localities were totally unfit for human habitation. Finding adequate solutions for these problems became a supreme challenge for Americans at the beginning of the twentieth century.

The first three parts of this book are designed to show how this challenge was met. The five writers in Part I express the most common responses. To these individuals the city was in essence a moral and political problem. When they observed its decadence, immorality and corruption, they felt compelled to expose them. Although primarily concerned only with diagnosing the existing problems, some of these writers advocated cures — a halt to urban growth, or a return to the smaller cities of an earlier era. The first selection, from one of Lord Bryce's speeches on the evils of great cities, argues that cities, by separating people from nature, become the breeding grounds for violence. Henry George also bemoans the fact that urban dwellers cannot commune with mother earth. The result, he writes, is mental, physical and moral decay. In the third selection Benjamin O. Flower moves from the general dilemma of the city to the specific, by vividly describing the moral depravity in Boston's saloon and red-light district. This selection is followed by Jacob Riis's detailed exposé of one of New York's tenement districts.

The final selection in Part I is from one of Lincoln Steffens' numerous articles demonstrating how corrupt politicians took advantage of the existing urban conditions.

Part II contains selections from writers who wanted to do more than just describe evils and immorality: in a sense they were idealistic crusaders who hoped to redeem the fallen city. And redemption, they believed, could come only through the ethical values of Protestant Christianity, or through its moral equivalent, rural virtues. The first selection is by Charles Loring Brace, who viewed the poor in the cities, especially foreigners, as "dangerous classes" who might revolt unless prevented by charity in the spirit of religion. To Josiah Strong, the best way to meet the challenge of the city was with a reconstructive form of Christianity. He believed that the city could be saved only by the institutional church, because both environment and character must be changed in any permanent reform. The third selection is from Robert Woods's *The City Wilderness: A Settlement Study*. Woods was convinced that charity work and philanthropic agencies were important, but alone, not enough. He saw a need for reestablishing in the city the friendly, personal and informal relationships of neighborhood life, bringing into the industrial city the village concepts of community and hard work. Like Robert Woods, Jane Addams was a settlement house worker concerned about the disappearance of an older sense of community in the city. Here she calls for wholesome places for young people to meet — a "substitute for the old dances on the village green."

The selections in Part III demonstrate still another way that Americans met the challenge of the city. Rather than merely expose the evils of urban life, or impose older virtues on the city-dwellers, these authors sought ways to improve the city in terms of its own cultural and political advantages. The first selection, from two of William Dean Howells' utopian novels, acknowledges the intellectual and cultural rewards of urban living — especially for writers, artists and musicians. Rather than sacrifice these obvious advantages by doing away with cities completely, he suggests instead extensive city planning, patterned after the White City at the World's Columbian Exposition at Chicago in 1893. Dana Bartlett was no anti-urbanist, either. Firmly convinced that Los Angeles was the ideal city mostly because of its climate, he urged the development of an even better city through improved living conditions and city beautification. Typical of the new breed of social scientist at the beginning of the twentieth century, Frederic C. Howe maintains that the problem of the city was not personal or ethical, but economic. To meet its challange he called for a new perspective — a plan for the "whole community." Finally, he placed himself on the pole opposite to Lord Bryce; rather than decry the "great city as a great evil," he sanguinely envisioned it as the "hope of democracy."

Part IV, composed of selections by five contemporary students of the American city, analyzes the political, religious and cultural institutions of America from 1860 to the present. In the first selection Harvey Wish describes the way in which the modern city transformed the churches. Wish's article is followed by a selection from Christopher Tunnard's and Henry Hope Reed's *American Skyline*. They show that even in the period from 1880 to 1910, when rapid expansion

of the community was a primary concern, businessmen and architects had an eye for beauty. Indeed, some of our most venerated monuments and public buildings are legacies of that era. Roy Lubove analyzes the influence of such conceptions as "the garden city," "the city beautiful" and "the city useful" on city planning and housing activities during the Progressive era. In *The Era of Theodore Roosevelt, 1900–1912*, George E. Mowry maintains that through municipal reform organizations the city became "the inspirer of social democracy and . . . the originator of social regulation" in the twentieth century. In the final essay, Carl N. Degler maintains that beginning in the 1890's with the rise of the modern city, and continuing down to the 1960's, the urban voter has been the decisive factor in making one of the two major political parties the majority party.

The challenge of the city, of course, is still with us. Problems such as transportation, housing and the poverty of ghetto life have not been solved to this day. Indeed, these problems have grown more complex because of urban sprawl and the decay of the central city. Likewise, as urbanization continues, new problems such as air pollution and racial violence have emerged to challenge urban leaders. On the other hand, cities provide economic opportunity; they are seats of the industries which have given the United States her industrial supremacy.

So the debate continues. Some people still see the great cities as great evils. Others, however, devote their careers to the challenge of the city because they believe that it is the hope of democracy and therefore the hope of the future.

CONTENTS

I. THE CITY AS A MORAL AND POLITICAL PROBLEM

Lord (James) Bryce: THE MENACE OF GREAT CITIES

Lord Bryce, a respected British scholar and observer of American life and institutions, is well-remembered for stating in his book, The American Commonwealth, *that "the government of cities is the one conspicuous failure of the United States." Actually, Bryce had few compliments for any aspect of the urban scene. In this speech, delivered to a housing conference in New York, he outlines the evils of cities and urges businessmen to move their industries into smaller communities.*

I WISH to give you some reasons why a great city is a great evil.

First: From the point of view of health. In the city, and most of the great cities are crowded, there must be less oxygen and more microbes. I believe it is a fact that no city has maintained itself and its standard of physical excellence without an indraught from the country. If you were to leave the city alone, stop the indraught of the people who have grown up and formed their constitutions in the air of the country, the population would decline physically and, perhaps, begin to die out.

Second: It is a great evil in the city that people are cut off from nature and communion with nature, so that they who would like to enjoy the sights and scenes and blessings of nature can do so only on rare occasions and by taking a journey.

Third: It is an evil in that it separates the greater part of the community into classes and disturbs the sentiment of neighborliness between the richer and the poorer, which existed formerly in smaller communities, and which ought to exist. You have endeavored to remedy that in your great cities by founding what are called Settlements, where a few members of the wealthy class go down and live among the members of the poorer class and try to help them. That is very excellent and wholesome, a very valuable remedy, but, after all, it is only palliative. It would be better for the community not only that the wealthier classes should have the other classes constantly in sight, but that neighborly relations of human fellowship could more naturally be cultivated, because they dwelt near at hand.

Fourth: Life in the great city tends to stimulate and increase beyond measure that which is the menace of the American city — intensification of nervous strain and nervous excitability. Cities are the homes — especially in the United States — of every kind of noise, and nothing in the long run puts a greater strain on the nervous system than incessant noise. People live in crowds, under the ceaseless stimulus of always seeing one another in crowds, always moving to and fro in street cars and railroads and automobiles, backwards and forwards at an increasing rate of speed. They are always under

From Lord (James) Bryce, "The Menace of Great Cities," *Housing Problems in America, Proceedings of the Second National Conference on Housing* (Cambridge, Mass., 1912), pp. 17–22.

that exciting influence which the mere sense of living in a crowd of people and of trying to pack so many things in the twenty-four hours, including the reading of numerous newspapers, produces. It tells injuriously upon the nervous system. All these things tend to increase the nervous excitability and the consequent neurasthenia from which we are told most of us are suffering. Some people think this is going to be the real danger in the future of the human race, and that unless the right means are found for the protection of our nervous system, its undue stimulation and consequent exhaustion may become a source of weakness for mankind.

Fifth: If these conditions are not favorable for the population generally, they are particularly unfavorable for the bairns – I mean the boys and girls. The boy living in the country has any amount of opportunity for the development of his vitality, full space to give vent to his natural exuberance of energy. He climbs trees, jumps over fences, throws stones at the birds – fortunately he does not usually hit them; he rambles about with his boy companions and gathers blackberries and sees all kinds of things upon which his natural activity expends itself. He has all sorts of winter sports in snow and on ice. So he gets insight into nature through his curiosity and can have in the country some little sense of adventure. But if he is cooped up in the city he takes to rambling the street at night with other boys, and if he is not well guided in his home he is very apt to fall into bad company and get into all sorts of trouble. I think the Boy Scout movement has done a great deal to meet and cure that danger, but still it is a danger for many boys. There has grown up in the large cities a class for whom names have been invented, like "hoodlums" in California, and "larrikins" in Australia, which denote an undesirable kind of boy citizen. It is a tendency much in evidence in huge cities among the younger part of the community, who have a superabundance of energy which cannot work itself off in the old natural way.

Sixth: Great cities are liable to become great dangers in a political sense, because the more men are crowded in great masses, the more easily they become excited, the more they are swept away by words, and the more they form what might be called a revolutionary temper. All revolutionary movements or acts of violence are more apt to spring up in a dense city population, a population which is liable to be swept by excess of emotions, than among people living in the country.

Lastly: In the great city there is a deplorable amount of economic waste. In the city the manufactories, offices, warehouses and shops, all the large places in which people are employed, whether in distributing commodities or purchasing, are in the central parts of the city. The people want to live in the outer parts of the city, and as the city grows the people are driven more and more into the outskirts. If you will consider the amount of time that is taken from work to be given to mere transportation from the residence of the workingman to his working place in the city, you will see how great the loss is.

I used to make computations of that in London. In London a large part of our working people live on the eastern side of London, the northern side and the southwest, and come in ten, twelve or fourteen miles every day to work. The man walks ten minutes to the railway station from the place where he lives, and then walks another ten minutes from the station to his work in the city, and he spends from three-quarters of an hour to fifty minutes, sometimes perhaps as much as sixty minutes, on the railroad. In other words he wastes from fifty to seventy minutes in the morning, and as much in the evening, which might be given to work, or if not to work, then to mental recreation or improvement.

Think what that means in a year. Think what is the waste that is involved in a great city like London or New York in people spending an hour or more in the morning and another hour or more in the evening in going to and fro to their work, when if they were near their work they might either be working or enjoying themselves or having wholesome rest. It is an economic waste which is really an insult to our civilization; it ought to appeal to us on the mere business side, the need for saving the productive capacity of our people from such waste.

Now, what can you do about it? I am told that there are obvious advantages in great cities. No doubt there is an advantage in that you can have a certain amount of pleasure. You can have better libraries, finer museums and zöological and botanical gardens on a larger scale. You can have larger and more varied commercial interests and a fuller social life, and you can have a far greater choice of amusements, more music, more plays in the theater.

The business man says he must be where the greatest facilities for transportation exist, namely, where the largest number of railroads converge, and the place where he can have the largest supply of labor at short notice, and where he can get any kind of labor that he wants

because there is a large floating population.

I do not deny that there is force in all this. But at the same time even the business man will surely admit that it ought to be a great advantage to him in the smaller place to be able to get land very much cheaper. There he can lay out his factory building on approved lines and provide not only larger spaces for his works but also larger and more convenient dwellings for his workingmen.

Of course we all believe that business looks after itself, that men know better their own business than anybody else could tell them. At the same time I do believe that there are cases where men go by rule of thumb, merely doing as other people have done, merely following in a trodden path, without stopping to think that it is worth while to give attention to those considerations which sometimes occur to us who look at things in a theoretical as well as a practical way. You all know that in matters of shop management suggestions of great value have been recently put forward by Mr. Frederick Taylor, which have attracted much attention, and I believe are being taken advantage of, which will effect a great saving of economic waste. These suggestions might have occurred to many other business men, but it was left to Mr. Taylor to think out the matter and show its importance. So, I am sure, there are many particulars of social mechanism in which it will be possible to remove waste if people would only begin to stop and think about it instead of blindly following in the pathways they have become accustomed to tread.

Henry George: CITY AND COUNTRY

The economist Henry George, like Lord Bryce, looked upon cities as destructive of health and morality. He is best remembered for his book, Progress and Poverty (1879), which sets forth the "single tax" theory alluded to in this article. One of the purposes of this tax on the unearned increment in land values was to dissolve the large cities and distribute population more naturally.

COBBETT compared London, even in his day, to a great wen growing upon the fair face of England. There is truth in such comparison. Nothing more clearly shows the unhealthiness of present social tendencies than the steadily increasing concentration of population in great cities. There are about 12,000 head of beef cattle killed weekly in the shambles of New York, while, exclusive of what goes through for export, there are about 2100 beef carcasses per week brought in refrigerator cars from Chicago. Consider what this single item in the food supply of a great city suggests as to the elements of fertility, which, instead of being returned to the soil from which they come, are swept out through the sewers of our great cities. The reverse of this is the destructive character of our agriculture, which is year by year decreasing the productiveness of our soil, and virtually lessening the area of land available for the support of our increasing millions.

In all the aspects of human life similar effects are being produced. The vast populations of these great cities are utterly divorced from all the genial influences of nature. The great mass of them never, from year's end to year's end, press foot upon mother earth, or pluck a wild flower, or hear the tinkle of brooks, the rustle of grain, or the murmur of leaves as the light breeze comes through the woods. All the sweet and joyous influences of nature are shut out from them. Her sounds are drowned by the roar of the streets and the clatter of the people in the next room, or the next tenement; her sights are hidden from their eyes by rows of high buildings. Sun and moon rise and set, and in solemn procession the constellations move across the sky, but these imprisoned multitudes behold them only as might a man in a deep quarry. The white snow falls in winter only to become dirty slush on the pavements, and as the sun sinks in summer a worse than noonday heat is refracted from masses of brick and stone. Wisely have the authorities of Philadelphia labeled with its name every tree in their squares; for how else shall the children growing up in such cities know one tree from another? how shall they even know grass from clover?

This life of great cities is not the natural life of man. He must, under such conditions, deteriorate, physically, mentally, morally. Yet the evil does not end here. This is only one side of it. This unnatural life of the great cities means an equally unnatural life in the country. Just as the wen or tumor, drawing the wholesome juices of the body into its poisonous vortex, impoverishes all other parts of the frame, so does the crowding

From Henry George, "City and Country," *The Complete Works of Henry George* (New York: Doubleday & McClure Co., 1898), Vol. III, pp. 234–240.

of human beings into great cities impoverish human life in the country.

Man is a gregarious animal. He cannot live by bread alone. If he suffers in body, mind and soul from being crowded into too close contact with his fellows, so also does he suffer from being separated too far from them. The beauty and the grandeur of nature pall upon man where other men are not to be met; her infinite diversity becomes monotonous where there is not human companionship; his physical comforts are poor and scant, his nobler powers languish; all that makes him higher than the animal suffers for want of the stimulus that comes from the contact of man with man. Consider the barrenness of the isolated farmer's life — the dull round of work and sleep, in which so much of it passes. Consider, what is still worse, the monotonous existence to which his wife is condemned; its lack of recreation and excitement, and of gratifications of taste, and of the sense of harmony and beauty; its steady drag of cares and toils that make women worn and wrinkled when they should be in their bloom. Even the discomforts and evils of the crowded tenement-house are not worse than the discomforts and evils of such a life. Yet as the cities grow, unwholesomely crowding people together till they are packed in tiers, family above family, so are they unwholesomely separated in the country. The tendency everywhere that this process of urban concentration is going on, is to make the life of the country poor and hard, and to rob it of the social stimulus and social gratifications that are so necessary to human beings. The old healthy social life of village and townland is everywhere disappearing. In England, Scotland and Ireland, the thinning out of population in the agricultural districts is as marked as is its concentration in cities and large towns. In Ireland, as you ride along the roads, your car-driver, if he be an old man, will point out to you spot after spot, which, when he was a boy, were the sites of populous hamlets, echoing in the summer evenings with the laughter of children and the joyous sports of young people, but now utterly desolate, showing, as the only evidences of human occupation, the isolated cabins of miserable herds. In Scotland, where in such cities as Glasgow, human beings are so crowded together that two-thirds of the families live in a single room, where if you go through the streets of a Saturday night, you will think, if you have ever seen the Tierra del Fuegans, that these poor creatures might envy them, there are wide tracts once populous, now given up to cattle, to grouse and to deer — glens that once sent out their thousand fighting men, now tenanted by a couple of gamekeepers. So across the Tweed, while London, Liverpool, Leeds, Manchester and Nottingham have grown, the village life of "merrie England" is all but extinct. Two-thirds of the entire population is crowded into cities. Clustering hamlets, such as those through which, according to tradition, Shakespeare and his comrades rollicked, have disappeared; village greens where stood the May-pole, and the cloth-yard arrow flew from the longbow to the bull's-eye of the butt, are plowed under or inclosed by the walls of some lordly demesne, while here and there stand mementos alike of a bygone faith and a departed population, in great churches or their remains — churches such as now could never be filled unless the congregations were brought from town by railroad excursion trains.

So in the agricultural districts of our older States the same tendency may be beheld; but it is in the newer States that its fullest expression is to be found — in ranches measured by square miles, where live half-savage cowboys, whose social life is confined to the excitement of the "round-up" or a periodical "drunk" in a railroad town; and in bonanza farms, where in the spring the eye wearies of seas of waving grain before resting on a single home — farms where the cultivators are lodged in barracks, and only the superintendent enjoys the luxury of a wife.

That present tendencies are hurrying modern society toward inevitable catastrophe, is apparent from the constantly increasing concentration of population in great cities, if in nothing else. A century ago New York and its suburbs contained about 25,000 souls; now they contain over 2,000,000. The same growth for another century would put here a population of 160,000,000. Such a city is impossible. But what shall we say of the cities of ten and twenty millions, that, if present tendencies continue, children now born shall see?

On this, however, I will not dwell. I merely wish to call attention to the fact that this concentration of population impoverishes social life at the extremities, as well as poisons it at the center; that it is as injurious to the farmer as it is to the inhabitant of the city.

This unnatural distribution of population, like that unnatural distribution of wealth which gives one man hundreds of millions and makes other men tramps, is the result of the action of the new industrial forces in social conditions not adapted to them. It springs primarily from our treatment of land as private property, and secondarily from our neglect to assume social functions which material progress forces upon us. Its causes removed, there would ensue a natural distribution of population, which would give every one breathing-space and neighborhood.

It is in this that would be the great gain of the farmer in the measures I have proposed. With the resumption of common rights to the soil, the overcrowded population of the cities would spread, the scattered population of the country would grow denser. When no individual could profit by advance in the value of land, when no one need fear that his children could be jostled out of their natural rights, no one would want more land than he could profitably use. Instead of scraggy, half-cultivated farms, separated by great tracts lying idle, homesteads would come close to each other. Emigrants would not toil through unused acres, nor grain be hauled for thousands of miles past half-tilled land. The use of machinery would not be abandoned: where culture on a large scale secured economies it would still go on; but with the breaking up of monopolies, the rise in wages and the better distribution of wealth, industry of this kind would assume the cooperative form. Agriculture would cease to be destructive, and would become more intense, obtaining more from the soil and returning what it borrowed. Closer settlement would give rise to economies of all kinds; labor would be far more productive, and rural life would partake of the conveniences, recreations and stimulations now to be obtained only by the favored classes in large towns. The monopoly of land broken up, it seems to me that rural life would tend to revert to the primitive type of the village surrounded by cultivated fields, with its common pasturage and woodlands. But however this may be, the working farmer would participate fully in all the enormous economies and all the immense gains which society can secure by the substitution of orderly cooperation for the anarchy of reckless, greedy scrambling.

That the masses now festering in the tenement-houses of our cities, under conditions which breed disease and death, and vice and crime, should each family have its healthful home, set in its garden; that the working farmer should be able to make a living with a daily average of two or three hours' work, which more resembled healthy recreation than toil; that his home should be replete with all the conveniences yet esteemed luxuries; that it should be supplied with light and heat, and power if needed, and connected with those of his neighbors by the telephone; that his family should be free to libraries, and lectures, and scientific apparatus, and instruction; that they should be able to visit the theater, or concert, or opera, as often as they cared to, and occasionally to make trips to other parts of the country or to Europe; that, in short, not merely the successful man, the one in a thousand, but the man of ordinary parts and ordinary foresight and prudence, should enjoy all that advancing civilization can bring to elevate and expand human life, seems, in the light of existing facts, as wild a dream as ever entered the brain of hashish-eater. Yet the powers already within the grasp of man make it easily possible.

In our mad scramble to get on top of one another, how little do we take of the good things that bountiful nature offers us! Consider this fact: to the majority of people in such countries as England, and even largely in the United States, fruit is a luxury. Yet mother earth is not niggard of her fruit. If we chose to have it so, every road might be lined with fruit-trees.

Benjamin O. Flower: CIVILIZATION'S INFERNO

An early muckraker and reformer, Benjamin O. Flower founded The Arena, *a leading radical magazine of the Gilded Age. This selection shows his concern for moral degradation in the city. As historian Charles N. Glaab has written, Flower "was shocked at the manifestation of evil but . . . showed little awareness of its cause."*

THERE is today in all populous centers of civilization a world of misery, where uninvited poverty abounds: a commonwealth of victims whose wretchedness fills the heart with mingled sorrow and indignation. No more pathetic scene can be imagined than the daily battle waged by this battalion in retreat, which yet struggles for a foothold on the granite of honesty and virtue. There is, however, another spectacle still more soul-sickening, because of its added blackness. Below the social cellar, where uninvited poverty holds sway, is a darker zone: a subterranean, rayless vault — the commonwealth of the double night. In the upper stratum we find gloom; here perpetual darkness. Above, the closing door of opportunity to live, the frightful pangs of hunger and the ever-present dread of sickness shut out the sunshine of external enjoyments; still, so long as virtue and integrity remain, the inner temple is illuminated. In the sub-cellar, however, even the soul's torch goes out; hence there is twofold darkness. So long as the fires burn on the altar of morality the soul knows an exalted pleasure, even in

From Benjamin O. Flower, *Civilization's Inferno* (Boston, 1893), pp. 99–109.

the bitterest want; for the mystic power of the Divine, impearled in every mind, holds supremacy, and the spirit stands erect. When, however, this light disappears, the soul grovels in the mire, and the incentive to walk is less strong than that to crawl and wallow in animality. In this underworld vice and crime mingle with poverty; bestial passion is the goddess of its denizens; here the acme of pleasure is reached in sensual gratification; here men do not look you in the eye; the glance, even, is furtive when not defiant. *This is the real inferno.* No need to wander into other worlds for hells of God's creating. Man has made an underworld, before which the most daring imagination of poet or seer staggers. Over its portals might well be blazoned the soul-freezing inscription which Dante beheld as he entered the underworld.

If its inhabitants came hither voluntarily, their conditions might merit less concern, even though they would in no less degree be a menace to society. But the truth is, the large proportion are driven hither by relentless influences, over which they have no control; such, for example, as the cupidity and avarice of powerful individuals, the selfishness of a short-sighted and indifferent civilization, reinforced by the intangible but potent influence of heredity on the one hand, and the still more irresistible power of environment on the other.

And in this subterranean world, as in the world of hope, we find men, women and children plying their trades and eking out an existence as fate or inclination dictates. Here, however, schools, universities and libraries contribute little to the satisfaction of man's appetites and aspirations; but in their stead we find the omnipresent saloon, catering to all that is worst in frail humanity.

Yet it must not be understood that all

pleasure is exiled; a certain kind of enjoyment remains. It is a counterfeit coin, which, however, in the absence of that which is real, passes current. It possesses none of the pure essence which endures and is refining and elevating. Moreover, the pleasures known here consume the life of the votaries, and are mingled with bitterness which increases with each hour of indulgence. They end also in death, prefaced by an existence loathsome to even the depraved souls who reap their certain fruitage.

Would you glance at the pseudo-pleasures current in this lower zone of life? Come with us as we skirt this realm, and see what it has to offer to those who have recently crossed its threshold. We are in Boston, within rifle-shot of the gilded dome of the State House and the palaces of Beacon Hill, and yet we are entering this underworld. It is Monday night. At the station-house we are politely received by the officer in charge, who observes that we have chosen the worst night in the week. Saturday and Sunday, he explains, are always a kind of Saturnalia for numbers of people in this part of the city; but Monday there is little to be seen. These people are "resting" or "broke." While he is speaking, a drunken man is brought in – a searcher for pleasure and gratification, who losing reason, has been overtaken by the law. "Do you make many arrests daily?" we asked. "Oh, yes, here is the record: for Saturday, fifty-six cases, yesterday thirty-five, mostly drunkenness. Ah, here is the officer who will go with you." We set off, threading our way through a commonwealth of poverty and vice. Here are thousands of people herding in crowded quarters where dwelt, a few decades ago, the very elite of the "Hub."

We have now reached a nest of old buildings with an unsavory record. Here we find Negroes and whites mingling together. The creaking stairways are worn and carpeted with filth; the walls and ceilings blistered with the foul accretions of months and perhaps years. It is a noisy spot; snatches of low songs, oaths, coarse jests, and the savage voices of poor wretches whose brains are inflamed and tongues made thick with rum, meet our ears on every side. The air is heavy with odors of spoiled fish, decayed vegetables, smoke from old pipes, and stale beer. From one room loud and angry voices proceed, a note of fear mingled with a threatening tone; the room seems perfectly dark. With a quick movement the officer lifts the smoking lamp from a stool in the hall, and opens the door. The scene is sickening in the extreme, one of the most disgusting spectacles in the underworld, none the less terrible because it is common. A filthy den, occupied by a young girl whose career has not yet brought upon her unmistakable signs of debauchery, save in a certain expression of the eyes and a brazen smile, which speak volumes against the probability of restoration. She is probably a Creole. A wealth of black hair falls in great waves over her head; she has a deep olive complexion; neither her hair nor her features indicate Negro blood; a large head, arching brow, and eyes which once must have been extremely beautiful, for even yet, though slightly dimmed by dissipation, they are very expressive. On her countenance one detects something inexpressibly sad; the sunshine of girlishness blending with the shadow of vice. A few years before she must have been a remarkably beautiful child, richly endowed by nature with those physical charms so dear to womankind, and which today are a fortune to a maiden in easy circumstances. This girl, surrounded in early life by healthy influences, schooled

in virtue and given a fair chance would probably have graced society and added to the dignity of womanhood. But the accident of an unkind fate willed otherwise, and now we find her in a filthy den, the air of which is heavy with fumes of liquor and other nauseous odors — her companion a low-browed, thick-necked Negro. Heartsick we turn from this spectacle, too common to the officer to even call to his face a momentary shadow of disgust. In this child of a dark fate we see a type of thousands of poor girls who seem doomed to wed despair. They may have entered life in the social cellar, where they have never seen, with anything like clear-cut vision, the line of demarkation between right and wrong. They may have drifted to the city for the purpose of making an honest living, but have been driven into vice and crime, in order that soulless greed might flourish and they still live. Or they may belong to the commonwealth of betrayed maidens, who, being betrayed, have found all society's doors barred against them, lest, perchance, they contaminate innocence, brush too closely against undiscovered sin, or annoy the lepers who have accomplished their ruin, and who still move unabashed in the upper world. In any case, to them birth was a calamity, life a bitter curse, death their sweetest heritage.

We leave this rookery, having caught a glimpse of life's sad quest for pleasure in the modern inferno, and traverse a street with brilliantly lighted saloons. The counters are thronged with scores of men, seeking pleasure by imbibing beer. At the corner of the street a striking picture is presented. In the front window of a large saloon sits a company of young men and girls, laughing hilariously over their liquor. The men are boyish in appearance. One of the three women present is not a novice. Her face is typical, and carries a significant history; brazen eyes, steeled and slightly dimmed; countenance stamped with the unmistakable history of reckless indulgence, doomed to grow more terrible as she is pushed, with ever accelerating speed, toward her frightful end. The features of the other girls show small traces of dissipation. They are well dressed; a rosy flush suffuses their brows, born of excitement rather than rouge; their voices also possess a silvery ring. They seem happy, as, with rapid words, jests pass from lip to lip over the clinking glasses.

Behind this partitioned compartment, the bar, thronged with men, is the scene of that coarse merriment which is ever found in saloons in low parts of great cities. We turn the corner, and passing the rear of the same establishment, catch another kaleidoscopic view of the pleasures of this dismal life. Here, in a rudely partitioned box, which partly shuts it from the bar, but which opens on the street, are a half-dozen withered women, some aged before their time; others, though still young, haggard and corpselike; their faces, like their ragged gowns, are faded, their voices harsh and rasping, their laugh barren of all merriment and carrying notes of defiance and despair. In the front of this saloon is laughing girlhood; in the rear besotted womanhood. The difference is that these poor creatures have pursued the *ignis-fatuus* a little longer than their younger neighbors – they are several rungs lower in the ladder – that is all. As we momentarily pause before this pathetic picture, one poor woman whose dull eyes are sunken far into their sockets, and whose face is of ashen hue, rises, and, extending her long fingers, beckons to our company. The grin on her face, which in childhood was doubtless a smile, is so ghastly that we are thrilled with horror. Ah! poor Ishmaelites of our nineteenth-century civilization, terrible is your fate!

Jacob Riis: THE TENEMENTS OF NEW YORK

Jacob Riis was one of the most widely read writers at the turn of the century. A police reporter, he associated closely with Theodore Roosevelt when the latter was head of New York's Board of Police Commissioners. His firsthand view of the deplorable living conditions of New York's poor inspired him to establish a settlement house there.

TODAY, what is a tenement? The law defines it as a house "occupied by three or more families, living independently and doing their cooking on the premises; or by more than two families on a floor, so living and cooking and having a common right in the halls, stairways, yards, etc." That is the legal meaning, and includes flats and apartment houses, with which we have nothing to do. In its narrower sense the typical tenement was thus described when last

From Jacob Riis, *How the Other Half Lives: Studies Among the Tenements of New York* (New York: Charles Scribner's Sons, 1890), pp. 17–20, 28–30, 43–47.

arraigned before the bar of public justice: "It is generally a brick building from four to six stories high on the street, frequently with a store on the first floor which, when used for the sale of liquor, has a side opening for the benefit of the inmates and to evade the Sunday law; four families occupy each floor, and a set of rooms consists of one or two dark closets, used as bedrooms, with a living room twelve feet by ten. The staircase is too often a dark well in the center of the house, and no direct through ventilation is possible, each family being separated from the other by partitions. Frequently the rear of the lot is occupied by another building of three stories high with two families on a floor." The picture is nearly as true today as ten years ago, and will be for a long time to come. The dim light admitted by the airshaft shines upon greater crowds than ever. Tenements are still "good property," and the poverty of the poor man his destruction. A barrack down town where he *has to live* because he is poor brings in a third more rent than a decent flat house in Harlem. The statement once made a sensation that between seventy and eighty children had been found in one tenement. It no longer excites even passing attention, when the sanitary police report counting 101 adults and 91 children in a Crosby Street house, one of twins, built together. The children in the other, if I am not mistaken, numbered 89, a total of 180 for two tenements! Or when a midnight inspection in Mulberry Street unearths a hundred and fifty "lodgers" sleeping on filthy floors in two buildings. Spite of brown-stone trimmings, plate-glass and mosaic vestibule floors, the water does not rise in summer to the second story, while the beer flows unchecked to the all-night picnics on the roof. The saloon with the side-door and the landlord divide the prosperity of the place between them, and the tenant, in sullen submission, foots the bills.

Where are the tenements of today? Say rather: where are they not? In fifty years they have crept up from the Fourth Ward slums and the Five Points the whole length of the island, and have polluted the Annexed District to the Westchester line. Crowding all the lower wards, wherever business leaves a foot of ground unclaimed; strung along both rivers, like ball and chain tied to the foot of every street, and filling up Harlem with their restless, pent-up multitudes, they hold within their clutch the wealth and business of New York, hold them at their mercy in the day of mob-rule and wrath. The bullet-proof shutters, the stacks of hand-grenades, and the Gatling guns of the Sub-Treasury are tacit admissions of the fact and of the quality of the mercy expected. The tenements today are New York, harboring three-fourths of its population. . . .

Down below Chatham Square, in the old Fourth Ward, where the cradle of the tenement stood, we shall find New York's Other Half at home, receiving such as care to call and are not afraid. Not all of it, to be sure, there is not room for that; but a fairly representative gathering, representative of its earliest and worst traditions. There is nothing to be afraid of. In this metropolis, let it be understood, there is no public street where the stranger may not go safely by day and by night, provided he knows how to mind his own business and is sober. His coming and going will excite little interest, unless he is suspected of being a truant officer, in which case he will be impressed with the truth of the observation that the American stock is dying out for want of children. If he escapes this suspicion and the risk of trampling upon, or being himself run down by the bewildering swarms of youngsters that are everywhere or nowhere as the exigency and their quick scent of danger direct, he will see no reason for dissenting from that observation. Glimpses caught of the parents watching the youngsters play from windows or open doorways will soon convince him that the native stock is in no way involved.

Leaving the Elevated Railroad where it dives under the Brooklyn Bridge at Franklin Square, scarce a dozen steps will take us where we wish to go. With its rush and roar echoing yet in our ears, we have turned the corner from prosperity to poverty. We stand upon the domain of the tenement. In the shadow of the great stone abutments the old Knickerbocker houses linger like ghosts of a departed day. Down the winding slope of Cherry Street — proud and fashionable Cherry Hill that was — their broad steps, sloping roofs, and dormer windows are easily made out; all the more easily for the contrast with the ugly barracks that elbow them right and left. These never had other design than to shelter, at as little outlay as possible, the greatest crowds out of which rent could be wrung. They were the bad afterthought of a heedless day. The years have brought to the old houses unhonored age, a querulous second childhood that is out of tune with the time, their tenants, the neighbors, and cries out against them and against you in fretful protest in every step on their rotten floors or squeaky stairs. Good cause have they for their fretting. This one, with its shabby front and poorly patched roof, what glowing firesides, what happy children may it once have owned? Heavy feet, too often with unsteady step, for the pot-house is next door — where is it not next door in these slums? — have worn away the brownstone steps since; the

broken columns at the door have rotted away at the base. Of the handsome cornice barely a trace is left. Dirt and desolation reign in the wide hallway, and danger lurks on the stairs. Rough pine boards fence off the roomy fireplaces — where coal is bought by the pail at the rate of twelve dollars a ton these have no place. The arched gateway leads no longer to a shady bower on the banks of the rushing stream, inviting to daydreams with its gentle repose, but to a dark and nameless alley, shut in by high brick walls, cheerless as the lives of those they shelter. The wolf knocks loudly at the gate in the troubled dreams that come to this alley, echoes of the day's cares. A horde of dirty children play about the dripping hydrant, the only thing in the alley that thinks enough of its chance to make the most of it: it is the best it can do. These are the children of the tenements, the growing generation of the slums; this their home. . . .

Suppose we look into one? No. — Cherry Street. Be a little careful, please! The hall is dark and you might stumble over the children pitching pennies back there. Not that it would hurt them; kicks and cuffs are their daily diet. They have little else. Here where the hall turns and dives into utter darkness is a step, and another, another. A flight of stairs. You can feel your way, if you cannot see it. Close? Yes! What would you have? All the fresh air that ever enters these stairs comes from the hall door that is forever slamming, and from the windows of dark bedrooms that in turn receive from the stairs their sole supply of the elements God meant to be free, but man deals out with such niggardly hand. That was a woman filling her pail by the hydrant you just bumped against. The sinks are in the hallway, that all the tenants may have access — and all be poisoned alike by their summer stenches. Hear the pump squeak! It is the lullaby of tenement-house babes. In summer, when a thousand thirsty throats pant for a cooling drink in this block, it is worked in vain. But the saloon, whose open door you passed in the hall, is always there. The smell of it has followed you up. Here is a door. Listen! That short hacking cough, that tiny, helpless wail — what do they mean? They mean that the soiled bow of white you saw on the door downstairs will have another story to tell — Oh! a sadly familiar story — before the day is at an end. The child is dying with measles. With half a chance it might have lived; but it had none. That dark bedroom killed it.

"It was took all of a suddint," says the mother, smoothing the throbbing little body with trembling hands. There is no unkindness in the rough voice of the man in the jumper, who sits by the window grimly smoking a clay pipe, with the little life ebbing out in his sight, bitter as his words sound: "Hush, Mary! If we cannot keep the baby, need we complain — such as we?"

Such as we! What if the words ring in your ears as we grope our way up the stairs and down from floor to floor, listening to the sounds behind the closed doors — some of quarrelling, some of coarse songs, more of profanity. They are true. When the summer heats come with their suffering they have meaning more terrible than words can tell. Come over here. Step carefully over this baby — it is a baby, spite of its rags and dirt — under these iron bridges called fire escapes but loaded down, despite the incessant watchfulness of the firemen, with broken household goods, with wash-tubs and barrels, over which no man could climb from a fire. This gap between dingy brick walls is the yard. That strip of smoke-colored sky up there is the heaven of these people. Do you wonder the name does not attract them to the churches? That baby's parents live in the rear tenement here. She is at least as clean as the steps we are now climbing. There are plenty of houses with half a hundred such in. The tenement is much like the one in front we just left, only fouler, closer, darker — we will not say more cheerless. The word is a mockery. A hundred thousand people lived in rear tenements in New York last year. Here is a room neater than the rest. The woman, a stout matron with hard lines of care in her face, is at the wash-tub. "I try to keep the childer clean," she says, apologetically, but with a hopeless glance around. The spice of hot soap-suds is added to the air already tainted with the smell of boiling cabbage, of rags and uncleanliness all about. It makes an overpowering compound. It is Thursday, but patched linen is hung upon the pulley-line from the window. There is no Monday cleaning in the tenements. It is wash-day all the week round, for a change of clothing is scarce among the poor. They are poverty's honest badge, these perennial lines of rags hung out to dry, those that are not the washerwoman's professional shingle. The true line to be drawn between pauperism and honest poverty is the clothes-line. With it begins the effort to be clean that is the first and the best evidence of a desire to be honest.

What sort of an answer, think you, would come from these tenements to the question "Is life worth living?" were they heard at all in the discussion? It may be that this, cut from the last report but one of the Association for the Improvement of the Condition of the Poor, a long name for a weary task, has a suggestion of it: "In the depth of winter the attention of the Association was called to a Protestant family living in a garret in a miserable tenement in Cherry Street. The family's condition was most deplorable. The man, his wife, and three small children shivering in one room through the roof of which the pitiless winds of winter whistled. The room was almost barren of furniture; the parents slept on the floor, the elder children in boxes, and the baby was swung in an old shawl attached to the rafters by cords by way of a hammock. The father, a seaman, had been obliged to give up that calling because he was in consumption, and was unable to provide either bread or fire for his little ones."

Perhaps this may be put down as an exceptional case, but one that came to my notice some months ago in a Seventh Ward tenement was typical enough to escape that reproach. There were nine in the family: husband, wife, an aged grandmother, and six children; honest, hard-working Germans, scrupulously neat, but poor. All nine lived in two rooms, one about ten feet square that served as parlor, bedroom, and eating-room, the other a small hall-room made into a kitchen. The rent was seven dollars and a half a month, more than a week's wages for the husband and father, who was the only bread-winner in the family. That day the mother had thrown herself out of the window, and was carried up from the street dead. She was "discouraged," said some of the other women from the tenement, who had come in to look after the children while a messenger carried the news to the father at the shop. They went stolidly about their task, although they were evidently not without feeling for the dead woman. No doubt she was wrong in not taking life philosophically, as did the four families a city missionary found housekeeping in the four corners of one room. They got along well enough together until one of the families took a boarder and made trouble. Philosophy, according to my optimistic friend, naturally inhabits the tenements. The people who live there come to look upon death in a different way from the rest of us — do not take it as hard. He has never found time to explain how the fact fits into his general theory that life is not unbearable in the tenements. Unhappily for the philosophy of the slums, it is too apt to be of the kind that readily recognizes the saloon, always handy, as the refuge from every trouble, and shapes its practice according to the discovery.

Lincoln Steffens: PHILADELPHIA — CORRUPT AND CONTENTED

One of the most famous muckrakers of the Progressive era was Lincoln Steffens. A prolific journalist, Steffens was unexcelled in understanding and explaining the abject corruption in city politics. As a reporter for McClure's Magazine, he wrote several articles on political corruption in major cities, a series which in 1902 was brought together in a volume entitled The Shame of the Cities. This selection describes in detail the political problems of Philadelphia near the turn of the century.

From Lincoln Steffens, "Philadelphia — Corrupt and Contented," *McClure's Magazine*, Vol. XXI (July, 1903), pp. 249–250, 253.

OTHER American cities, no matter how bad their own condition may be, all point with scorn to Philadelphia as worse — "the worst governed city in the country." St. Louis, Minneapolis, Pittsburg submit with some patience to the jibes of any other community; the most friendly suggestion from Philadelphia is rejected with contempt. The Philadelphians are "supine," "asleep"; hopelessly ring-ruled, they are "complacent." "Politically benighted," Philadelphia is supposed to have no light to throw upon a state of things that is almost universal.

This is not fair. Philadelphia is, indeed, corrupt; but it is not without significance. Every city and town in the country can learn something from the typical political experience of this great representative city. New York is excused for many of its ills because it is the metropolis, Chicago because of its forced development; Philadelphia is our "third largest" city and its growth has been gradual and natural. Immigration has been blamed for our municipal conditions; Philadelphia, with 47 per cent of the population native born of native born parents, is the most American of our greater cities. It is "good," too, and intelligent. I don't know how to measure the intelligence of a community, but a Pennsylvania college professor who declared to me his belief in education for the masses as a way out of political corruption, himself justified the "rake-off" of preferred contractors on public works on the ground of a "fair business profit." Another plea we have made is that we are too busy to attend to public business, and we have promised, when we come to wealth and leisure, to do better. Philadelphia has long enjoyed great and widely distributed prosperity; it is the city of homes; there is a dwelling house for every five persons, — men, women, and children, — of the population; and the people give one a sense of more leisure and repose than any community I ever dwelt in. Some Philadelphians account for their political state on the ground of their ease and comfort. There is another class of optimists whose hope is in an "aristocracy" that is to come by and by; Philadelphia is surer that it has a "real aristocracy" than any other place in the world, but its aristocrats with few exceptions are in the ring, with it, or of no political use. Then we hear that we are a young people and that when we are older and "have traditions," like some of the old countries, we also will be honest. Philadelphia is one of the oldest of our cities and treasures for us scenes and relics of some of the noblest traditions of our fair land. Yet I was told how once, for a joke, a party of boodlers counted out the "divvy" of their graft in unison with the ancient chime of Independence Hall.

Philadelphia is representative. This very "joke," told, as it was, with a laugh, is typical. All our municipal governments are more or less bad and all our people are optimists. Philadelphia is simply the most corrupt and the most contented. Minneapolis has cleaned up, Pittsburg has tried to, New York fights every other election, Chicago fights all the time. Even St. Louis has begun to stir (since the elections are over) and at the worst was only shameless. Philadelphia is proud; good people there defend corruption and boast of their machine. My college professor, with his philosophic view of "rake-offs," is one Philadelphia type. Another is the man who, driven to bay with his local pride, says: "At least you must admit that our machine is the best you have ever seen."

ALL THROUGH WITH REFORM

Disgraceful? Other cities say so. But I say that if Philadelphia is a disgrace, it is a disgrace not to itself alone, nor to Pennsylvania, but to the United States and to American character. For this great city, so highly representative in other respects, is not behind in political experience, but ahead, with New York. Philadelphia is a city that has had its reforms. Having passed through all the typical stages of corruption, Philadelphia reached the period of miscellaneous loot with a boss for chief thief, under James McManes and the Gas Ring 'way back in the late sixties and seventies. This is the Tweed stage of corruption from which St. Louis, for example, is just emerging. Philadelphia, in two inspiring popular revolts, attacked the Gas Ring, broke it, and in 1885 achieved that dream of American cities — a good charter. The present condition of Philadelphia, therefore, is not that which precedes, but that which follows reform, and in this distinction lies its startling general significance. What has happened since the Bullitt Law or charter went into effect in Philadelphia may happen in any American city "after reform is over."

For reform with us is usually revolt, not government, and is soon over. Our people do not seek, they avoid self rule, and "reforms" are spasmodic efforts to punish bad rulers and get somebody that will give us good government or something that will make it. A self-acting form of government is an ancient superstition. We are an inventive people and we all think that we shall devise some day a legal machine that will turn out good government automatically. The Philadelphians have treasured this belief longer than the rest of us and have tried it more often. Throughout their history they have sought this wonderful charter and they thought they had it when they got the Bullitt Law, which concentrates in the Mayor ample power, executive and political, and complete responsibility. Moreover, it calls for very little thought and action on the part of the people. All they expected to have to do when the Bullitt Law went into effect was to elect as Mayor a good business man, who with his probity and common sense would give them that good business administration which is the ideal of many reformers.

BUSINESS MEN AS MAYORS

The Bullitt Law went into effect in 1887. A committee of twelve — four from the Union League, four from business organizations, and four from the bosses — picked out the first man to run under it on the Republican ticket, Edwin H. Fitler, an able, upright business man, and he was elected. Strange to say, his administration was satisfactory to the citizens, who speak well of it to this day, and to the politicians also; Boss McManes (the ring was broken, not the boss) took to the next national convention from Philadelphia a delegation solid for Fitler for President of the United States. It was a farce, but it pleased Mr. Fitler, so Matthew S. Quay, the State boss, let him have a complimentary vote on the first ballot. The politicians "fooled" Mr. Fitler, and they "fooled" also the next business Mayor, Edwin S. Stuart, likewise a most estimable gentleman. Under these two administrations the foundation was laid for the present government of Philadelphia, the corruption to which Philadelphians seem so reconciled, and the machine which is "at least the best you have ever seen."

*   *   *

As I said in a previous article ("Tweed Days in St. Louis"), the politicians will learn, if the people won't, from exposure and reform. The Pennsylvania bosses learned the "uses of reform"; . . . Quay [applied] it to discipline McManes, and he since has turned reformer himself, to punish local bosses. The bosses have learned also the danger of combination between citizens and the Democrats. To prevent this, Quay and his friends have spread sedulously the doctrine of "reform within the party," and, from the Committee of One Hundred on, the reformers have stuck pretty faithfully to this principle. But lest the citizens should commit such a sin against their party, Martin formed a permanent combination of the Democratic with the Republican organization, using to that end a goodly share of the Federal and county patronage. Thus the people of Philadelphia were "fixed" so that they couldn't vote if they wanted to, and if they should want to, they couldn't vote for a Democrat, except of Republican or independent choosing. In other words, having taken away their ballot, the bosses took away also the choice of parties.

MAKING GRAFT SAFE

But the greatest lesson learned and applied was that of conciliation and "good government." The people must not want to vote or rebel against the ring. This ring, like any other, was formed for the exploitation of the city for private profit, and the cementing force is the "cohesive power of public plunder." But McManes and Tweed had proved that miscellaneous larceny was dangerous, and why should a lot of cheap politicians get so much and the people nothing at all? The people had been taught to expect but little from their rulers: good water, good light, clean streets well paved, fair transportation, the decent repression of vice, public order and public safety, and no scandalous or open corruption. It would be good business and good politics to give them these things. Like Chris Ma-

gee, who studied out the problem with him, Martin took away from the rank and file of the party and from the ward leaders and office holders the privilege of theft, and he formed companies and groups to handle the legitimate public business of the city. It was all graft, but it was to be all lawful, and, in the main, it was. Public franchises, public works, and public contracts were the principal branches of the business, and Martin adopted the dual boss idea which . . . [was] worked out by Magee and Flinn in Pittsburg. In Philadelphia it was Martin and Porter, and just as Flinn had a firm, Booth & Flinn, Ltd., so Porter was Filbert and Porter.

Filbert and Porter got all the public contracts they could handle, and the rest went to other contractors friendly to them and to the ring. Sometimes the preferred contractor was the lowest bidder, but he did not have to be. The law allowed awards to the "lowest and best," and the courts held that this gave the officials discretion. But since public criticism was to be considered, the ring, to keep up appearances, resorted to many tricks. One was to have fake bids made above the favorite. Another was to have the favorite bid high but set an impossible time limit; the department or the City Councils could extend the time afterwards. Still another was to arrange for specifications which would make outsiders bid high, then either openly alter the plans or let the ring firm perform work not up to requirements.

Many of Martin's deals and jobs were scandals, but they were safe; they were in the direction of public service; and the great mass of the business was done quietly. Moreover, the public was getting something for its money — not full value, but a good percentage. In other words, there was a limit to the "rake-off," and some insiders have told me that it had been laid down as a principle with the ring that the people should have in value (that is in work or benefit, including fair profit) ninety-five cents out of every dollar. In some of the deals I investigated, the "rake-off" over and above profit was as high as twenty-five per cent. Still, even at this, there was "a limit," and the public was getting, as one of the leaders told me, "a run for its money." Cynical as it all sounds, this view is taken by many Philadelphians almost if not quite as intelligent as my college professor.

II. THE REDEMPTION OF THE CITY

Charles Loring Brace: THE DANGEROUS CLASSES OF NEW YORK

> *One of the outspoken men who called for the redemption of the city
> in the Gilded Age was Charles Loring Brace. A leader in the Congre-
> gational Church and the Children's Aid Society, he viewed poverty as
> the city's most serious challenge. In this selection he warns that the
> poor are "dangerous classes" who may revolt, and he outlines his pre-
> ventive plan of Christian charity supported by state aid.*

NEW YORK is a much younger city
than its European rivals; and with
perhaps one-third the population of London, yet it presents varieties of life among
the "masses" quite as picturesque, and
elements of population even more dangerous. The throng of different national-
ities in the American city gives a pecu-
liarly variegated air to the life beneath
the surface, and the enormous overcrowding in portions of the poor quarters
intensifies the evils, peculiar to large
towns, to a degree seen only in a few
districts in such cities as London and
Liverpool.

The *mass* of poverty and wretchedness
is, of course, far greater in the English
capital. There are classes with inherited
pauperism and crime more deeply
stamped in them, in London or Glasgow,
than we ever behold in New York; but
certain small districts can be found in
our metropolis with the unhappy fame
of containing more human beings packed
to the square yard, and stained with more
acts of blood and riot, within a given
period, than is true of any other equal
space of earth in the civilized world.

There are houses, well known to sanitary boards and the police, where Fever
has taken a perennial lease, and will obey
no legal summons to quit; where Cholera
— if a single germ-seed of it float anywhere in American atmosphere — at once
ripens a black harvest; where Murder has
stained every floor of its gloomy stories,
and Vice skulks or riots from one year's
end to the other. Such houses are never
reformed. The only hope for them is in
the march of street improvements, which
will utterly sweep them away.

It is often urged that the breaking-up
of these "dens" and "fever-nests" only
scatters the pestilence and moral disease,
but does not put an end to them.

The objection is more apparent than
real. The abolishing of one of these centers of crime and poverty is somewhat
like withdrawing the virus from one dis-
eased limb and diffusing it through an
otherwise healthy body. It seems to lose
its intensity. The diffusion weakens.
Above all, it is less likely to become
hereditary.

One of the remarkable and hopeful
things about New York, to a close observer of its "dangerous classes," is, as
I shall show in a future chapter, that they
do not tend to become fixed and inherited, as in European cities.

But, though the crime and pauperism
of New York are not so deeply stamped

From Charles Loring Brace, *The Dangerous Classes of New York and Twenty Years' Work Among
Them* (New York: Wynkoop & Hallenbeck, Publishers, 1872), pp. 25–29, 74–76, 446–447.

in the blood of the population, they are even more dangerous. The intensity of the American temperament is felt in every fiber of these children of poverty and vice. Their crimes have the unrestrained and sanguinary character of a race accustomed to overcome all obstacles. They rifle a bank, where English thieves pick a pocket; they murder, where European *prolétaires* cudgel or fight with fists; in a riot, they begin what seems about to be the sacking of a city, where English rioters would merely batter policemen, or smash lamps. The "dangerous classes" of New York are mainly American-born, but the children of Irish and German immigrants. They are as ignorant as London flash-men or costermongers. They are far more brutal than the peasantry from whom they descend, and they are much banded together, in associations, such as "Dead Rabbit," "Plug-ugly," and various target companies. They are our *enfants perdus*, grown up to young manhood. The murder of an unoffending old man, like Mr. Rogers, is nothing to them. They are ready for any offense or crime, however degraded or bloody. New York has never experienced the full effect of the nurture of these youthful ruffians as she will one day. They showed their hand only slightly in the riots during the war. At present, they are like the athletes and gladiators of the Roman demagogues. They are the "roughs" who sustain the ward politicians, and frighten honest voters. They can "repeat" to an unlimited extent, and serve their employers. They live on "*panem et circenses*," or City-Hall places and pot-houses, where they have full credit.

. . . We may say in brief that the young ruffians of New York are the products of accident, ignorance, and vice. Among a million people, such as compose the population of this city and its suburbs, there will always be a great number of misfortunes; fathers die, and leave their children unprovided for; parents drink, and abuse their little ones, and they float away on the currents of the street; step-mothers or step-fathers drive out, by neglect and ill-treatment, their sons from home. Thousands are the children of poor foreigners, who have permitted them to grow up without school, education, or religion. All the neglect and bad education and evil example of a poor class tend to form others, who, as they mature, swell the ranks of ruffians and criminals. So, at length, a great multitude of ignorant, untrained, passionate, irreligious boys and young men are formed, who become the "dangerous class" of our city. They form the "Nineteenth-street Gangs," the young burglars and murderers, the garroters and rioters, the thieves and flash-men, the "repeaters" and ruffians, so well known to all who know this metropolis.

THE DANGERS

It has been common, since the recent terrible Communistic outbreak in Paris, to assume that France alone is exposed to such horrors; but, in the judgment of one who has been familiar with our "dangerous classes" for twenty years, there are just the same explosive social elements beneath the surface of New York as of Paris.

There are thousands on thousands in New York who have no assignable home, and "flit" from attic to attic, and cellar to cellar; there are other thousands more or less connected with criminal enterprises; and still other tens of thousands, poor, hard-pressed, and depending for daily bread on the day's earnings, swarming in tenement-houses, who behold the gilded rewards of toil all about them, but are never permitted to touch them.

All these great masses of destitute, miserable, and criminal persons believe that for ages the rich have had all the good things of life, while to them have been left the evil things. Capital to them is the tyrant.

Let but Law lift its hand from them for a season, or let the civilizing influences of American life fail to reach them, and, if the opportunity offered, we should see an explosion from this class which might leave this city in ashes and blood.

* * *

ORGANIZATION OF A REMEDY

In New York, we believe almost alone among the great capitals of the world, a profound and sustained effort for many years has been made to cut off the sources and diminish the numbers of the dangerous classes; and, as the records of crime show, with a marked effect.

In most large cities, the first practical difficulty is the want of a united organization to work upon the evils connected with this lowest class. There are too many scattered efforts, aiming in a desultory manner at this and that particular evil, resulting from the condition of the children of the streets. There is no unity of plan and of work. Every large city should form one Association or organization, whose sole object should be to deal alone with the sufferings, wants, and crimes, arising from a class of youth who are homeless, ignorant, or neglected. The injuries to public morals and property from such a class are important enough to call out the best thought and utmost energy and inventiveness of charitable men and women to prevent them. Where an association devotes itself thus to one great public evil, a thousand remedies or ingenious devices of cure and prevention

will be hit upon, when, with a more miscellaneous field of work, the best methods would be overlooked. So threatening is the danger in every populous town from the children who are neglected, that the best talent ought to be engaged to study their condition and devise their improvement, and the highest character and most ample means should be offered to guarantee and make permanent the movements devised for their elevation.

The lack of all this in many European capitals is a reason that so little, comparatively, has been done to meet these tremendous dangers.

Then, again, in religious communities, such as the English and American, there is too great a confidence in *technical religious* means.

We would not breathe a word against the absolute necessity of Christianity in any scheme of thorough social reform. If the Christian Church has one garland on its altars which time does not wither nor skepticism destroy, which is fresh and beautiful each year, it is that humble offering laid there through every age by the neglected little ones of society, whom the most enlightened Stoicism despised and Paganism cast out, but who have been blessed and saved by its ministrations of love. No skeptical doubt or "rationalism" can ever pluck from the Christian Church this, its purest crown.

To attempt to prevent or cure the fearful moral diseases of our lowest classes without Christianity, is like trying to carry through a sanitary reform in a city without sunlight.

But the mistake we refer to is a too great use of, or confidence in, the old technical methods — such as distributing tracts, and holding prayer-meetings, and scattering Bibles. The neglected and ruffian class which we are considering are in no way affected directly by such influences as these. New methods must be invented for them.

* * *

THE SECTARIAN DANGER

One rock, which the manager of such a movement must always steer clear of, is the sectarian difficulty. He must ignore sects, and rest his enterprise on the broadest and simplest principles of morality and religion. The animating force must be the religious, especially the "enthusiasm of humanity" shown in the love for Christ, and for all who bear His image. But dogmatic teachings, and disputations, and sectarian ambitions, are to be carefully eschewed and avoided in such efforts of humanity. The public must learn gradually to associate the movement, not with any particular sect or church, but with the feeling of humanity and religion — the very spirit of Christ Himself.

An essential thing, and often very disagreeable, to the earnest workers in it, is to give the utmost publicity to all its operations. The reason of this is that such a charity depends for support and friends, not on an organized private association, but on the whole public. They need to know all its doings; this is often the only way of reminding them of their duty in this field. Moreover, the moneys spent are public trust and all that relates to their uses should be publicly known.

CONCLUSION

Gradually, by publicity, the general community come to have something of the same moral interest in the enterprise, that the special attendants of a church have in its welfare; and it becomes a truly public interest. To attain this, the press should be the great agency, as well as the pulpit, wherever practicable. Annual reports, designed for all classes, wherein there are figures for the statistical, facts for the doubting, incidents for the young, and principles stated for the thoughtful, should be scattered far and wide.

As the organization grows, State aid should be secured for a portion of its expenses, that a more permanent character may be given it, and it may not be suddenly too much crippled by a business depression or disaster.

Of the modes in which money should be raised, . . . the general rule of wisdom is to avoid "sensation," and to trust to the settled and reasonable conviction of the public, rather than to temporary feeling or excitement.

Founded on such principles, and guided by men of this character and ability, and by those of similar purposes who shall come after them, there seems no good reason why this extended Charity should not scatter its blessings for generations to come throughout this ever-increasing metropolis.

Josiah Strong: THE CHALLENGE OF THE CITY

Josiah Strong, like Charles Loring Brace, hoped to redeem the city through Christian virtues. A leader in the Social Gospel movement, he believed that, although science could help save the city, a "socialized church" was the best solution to urban problems.

SHELLEY said: "Hell is a city much like London"; but the Revelator used a redeemed city to symbolize heaven — heaven come down to earth — the kingdom fully come.

Even if no solution of the problem of the city has yet been found, every one who believes that the prophetic prayer of our Lord, "thy kingdom come," is to receive its fulfilling answer must have confidence that the problem is soluble.

That the solution has really been found may be declared with all the confidence which springs from actual experience. Says Dr. Albert Shaw:

The abolition of the slums, and the destruction of their virus, are as feasible as the drainage of a swamp and the total dissipation of its miasmas. The conditions and circumstances that surround the lives of the masses of people in modern cities can be so adjusted to their needs as to result in the highest development of the race, in body, in mind, and in moral character. The so-called problems of the modern city are but the various phases of the one main question, How can the environment be most perfectly adapted to the welfare of urban populations? And science can meet and answer every one of these problems.

In enumerating the various branches of theoretical and practical knowledge on which the science of the modern city draws, Dr. Shaw specifies administrative science, statistical science, engineering and technological science, sanitary science, and educational, social, and moral science. Each of these is efficient, but all together they are not sufficient. They are all necessary, but they are not all that is necessary. The problem will not be solved until the city is saved, and the city will not be saved without religion.

As has been shown, the problem has two factors, — the environment and the people, — *both* of which must be changed. Some say, "Transform environment, and you will transform character"; while others say, "Transform the inner life, and the man will transform his surroundings." These are theories, both of which are disproved by actual experience.

In isolated instances men and women of the slum have been changed by divine grace. They now loathe many things they once loved, and naturally seek different associations, especially if they have children. If the old surroundings remain the same, if there is no refuge from temptation, if they must fight the habits of the old life single-handed, the chances are overwhelmingly against them.

On the other hand, municipal governments have, in some instances, condemned and destroyed the rookeries of large slum areas and have replaced them with model tenements. The London County Council has recently spent or is now spending $100,000,000 in this way; but investigation shows that the admirable new dwellings have not helped the

From Josiah Strong, *The Challenge of the City* (New York, 1907), pp. 199–202, 208–218. Reprinted by permission of the Young People's Missionary Movement.

class they were intended to help, have not saved those that needed saving. The sanitary cottages and airy flats have been occupied by comparatively well-to-do people, and the inmates of the former rookeries have been driven to others, which have become still more crowded. "Is there any light in Whitechapel for all this? Not a ray. In those frightful regions is no whit less misery, no less suffering, no fewer dwellers in the sub-cellars and dark alleys, no fewer stunted lives. Fewer? There are more."

In a word, improve the people without improving the environment, and they simply move away. We have saved individuals, but have not mitigated the slum, which remains to engulf others. Improve the environment without improving the people, and it is found that they are supplanted by a better class. The former occupants have not been uplifted, but have gone to aggravate slum conditions elsewhere.

It would be superfluous to argue with those for whom this book is written that religion is necessary to the salvation of the city. That goes without saying. We believe that the New Jerusalem comes down "from God." But in order to bring religion to bear for the salvation of the people, it is not enough that we address our efforts to the spiritual life and neglect the physical. The Master cared for both, and so must we.

* * *

The world is dying of selfishness, of which love is the only antidote. The commonest and most hopeless skepticism is disbelief in disinterested love, which alone is divine love. In order to convince the selfish world of disinterestedness, love must utter itself in something more than words. Service is its mother tongue. But in the commercial world service has its price; hence it does not always convince,

even when love is its motive. Only when service costs sacrifice does it overwhelm unbelief; and when sacrifice has convinced of human love, it has begun to reveal divine love.

The . . . principles of Christian work, briefly discussed, are all embodied and exemplified in the spirit and methods of the socialized or so-called institutional churches and of the religious social settlements. Let us look at them more closely.

SOCIALIZED CHURCHES

A church of this type has an enthusiasm for service.

Inasmuch as the Christ came not to be ministered unto, but to minister, the open and institutional church, filled and moved by his spirit of ministering love, seeks to become the center and source of all beneficent and philanthropic effort, and to take the leading part in every movement which has for its end the alleviation of human suffering, the elevation of man, and the betterment of the world.

Thus the open and institutional church aims to have all men and all of the man by all means, abolishing so far as possible the distinction between the religious and the secular, and sanctifying all ways and all means to the great end of saving the world for Christ.

A distinguishing characteristic of the socialized church is that it adapts itself to the needs of the local environment. In the tenement-house district,

It finds that the people living around it have in their homes no opportunity to take a bath; it therefore furnishes bathing facilities. It sees that the people have little or no healthful social life; it accordingly opens attractive social rooms, and organizes clubs for men, women, boys, and girls. The people know little of legitimate amusement; the church therefore provides it. They are ignorant of household economy; the church establishes its cooking-schools, its sewing-classes, and the like. In their homes the people have few books and papers; in the church they find a free reading-room and library. The homes afford no opportunity for intellectual cultivation; the church opens evening schools and provides lecture courses. As in the human organism, when one organ fails, its functions are often undertaken and more or less imperfectly performed by some other organ; so in the great social organism of the city, when the home fails, the church sometimes undertakes its functions.

Heretofore the church has addressed itself to the inner life and left the home to supply a healthy environment; but this the congested tenement cannot do; the socialized church therefore provides certain home conditions which are absolutely essential to normal life and growth.

A large proportion of the young people living around Berkeley Temple, Boston, came from country homes. When asked why they wished to join that church rather than some other, five out of six replied, "Because it is a home to me."

There is no better illustration of a socialized church adapting itself to the varied needs of the heterogeneous population of an American city than that afforded by St. Bartholomew's of New York City.

The schedule of services, classes, and clubs, and meetings of all sorts for every day in the week shows a total of 8,496 during the year, of which 1,422 are distinctly religious. Thus there are more services *rendered* than "held." The average number of gatherings on Sunday is 19, while the average for every week day in the year is 24. Sunday services are held in German, Swedish, Armenian, and Chinese, as well as English.

Under the assimilating influence of the Parish House, foreigners are being Americanized. An Armenian helper writes, "I am proud to say that as a good citizen I taught 21 Armenians the United States Constitution." Rescue mission work, with its nightly meetings, has been a prominent feature of the Parish House. The aggregate attendance on these meetings has been as large as 120,000 in a year, and 5,000 have professed to seek the new life.

The total number of communicants (1906) is 2,952. In the several Sunday schools there are 1,722 teachers and scholars. There are 336 members of the industrial school, 250 children in the kindergarten, and 2,796 members of the clubs for men, boys, and girls.

Membership in the Girls' Evening Club entitles the holder to "the use of the clubrooms and library; access to the large hall every evening after nine o'clock, to the physical culture classes, lectures, talks, entertainments, discussion class, glee club, literature class, English composition class, the Helping Hand Society, Penny Provident and Mutual Benefit Funds; the privilege of joining one class a week in either dressmaking, millinery, embroidery, drawn-work, system sewing, or cooking, and also, by paying a small fee, the privilege of entering a class in stenography, typewriting, French, or bookkeeping." Corresponding advantages attend membership in the other clubs.

A unique feature of the Parish House is its Roof Garden, on the top of nine busy stories. In long boxes the children plant flowers and vegetables. These have a background of lilac-bushes, syringa, and other flowering shrubs in large tubs: while morning-glories, honeysuckle, and ivy climb on the fence which surrounds the roof. The garden is used for the instruction and amusement of the children in the kindergarten when the weather permits, and is open evenings to various societies.

The Fresh Air work gave outings last summer to some 1,700 children and tired mothers. The Tailor Shop provides temporary work for many out of employment and supplies garments for children in the Sunday-schools and the Industrial school.

The report of the Penny Provident Fund shows 4,421 depositors and $31,485.29 deposited for 1906. One of the most beneficent of St. Bartholomew's many ministries is the Employment Bureau, which is conducted on business principles. During the year 1906 positions were found for 2,531 applicants. The largest number of situations filled in a single year was 5,200.

Another admirable institution is the Loan Association which has saved many from falling into the clutches of Shylock. Like the Employment Bureau, it is conducted strictly on business principles. The total receipts and loans for 1906 amounted to $192,862.59. The receipts and loans for the last eight years aggregate $1,373,531. The net earnings of the Association for 1906 were $3,546.25. The largest number of loans for a single year was 1,062.

Clinics,—medical, surgical, dental, eye, ear, throat, and nose, — are held daily except Sundays. Over 50,000 cases were treated during 1906.

The Loan, Employment, and Clothing Bureaus are open daily except Sundays; and are practically kept open all day excepting half a day on Saturdays.

The many-handed benefactions of the Parish House are maintained at an annual outlay of ninety to a hundred thousand dollars.

There are 249 salaried workers, including 7 clergymen, 1 deaconess, 3 parish visitors, 9 kindergartners, 25 instructors in clubs, 21 teachers, 1 physician, 6 nurses, 35 porters, cleaners, and laundresses, and 9 cooks and helpers.

There are also 896 volunteer workers, including 104 officers and teachers in Sunday-schools, 14 officers and teachers in the Industrial school, and 54 physicians.

St. Bartholomew's Parish Year Book is one of the best works on the *evidences of Christianity* — the Christianity of Christ — which it has ever been the privilege of the writer to read.

While large sums of money may be wisely expended by the socialized church, the experience of Morgan Chapel, Boston, shows that it is possible to do a varied and genuine social work and yet approximate self-support. In addition to the Sunday contributions, only $3,180 was required to provide fuel, lights, janitor's service, pastor's salary, and assistants for a year. The Chapel supplies baths, free concerts, and instruction in vocal and instrumental music. It has a school of handicrafts where printing, cobbling, tailoring, dressmaking, and carpentry are taught by volunteer instructors. It has an employment bureau, a medical mission, day nursery, kindergarten, and a children's industrial school.

The pastor writes: "Many churches hesitate to undertake any institutional church methods for fear of the great expense involved. The success that has attended the introduction of new methods at Morgan Chapel, and the small increase in the expenses of the work, may encourage others in similarly difficult fields to venture in like directions."

Two criticisms of the socialized church are sometimes made by those who lack sympathy with its aims or knowledge of its methods, which require some attention. It is said that such a church, well supplied with money, is in danger of pauperizing the community. It is true, as Emerson says, that "every man is as lazy as he dares to be"; and some men dare so much in that direction that it is perilously easy to pauperize them. Pauperizing the poor is as possible, as evil, and as inexcusable in the case of a socialized church as in the case of any other philanthropic institution; but such a result, if it takes place, is not necessary to institutional methods, but incidental to their administration.

The pastor of Morgan Chapel writes: "With less than $1,000 in cash to be used in poor relief last year, Morgan Memorial was able to extend help in the hour of their great need to 1,360 different families. These persons earned about $5,000 which was paid to them in fuel, groceries, clothing, and other supplies. They were not treated as paupers, for they earned what they got."

There is an annual average of more than a thousand "human derelicts" who by means of the industrial training at Morgan Memorial are taught self-respect through self-support.

Dr. William G. Partridge of Pittsburg, Pennsylvania, writes: "I have seen many men converted to the love and service of Christ, because the men's club had secured them employment through its employment committee. A church can carry on a great and diversified institutional work without giving away a dollar in money to the poor."

The other objection to the socialized church is that its activities in behalf of physical, intellectual, and social needs must detract from spiritual results. This would doubtless be true if the work were not inspired by the religious motive; but when spiritual results are the supreme aim, it is found that these methods are more productive of spiritual fruit than any others.

Of course there are no exact measurements of spiritual results; but the number of additions on confession of faith constitutes the best we have. It should be remarked, however, that such a comparison is hardly fair to the socialized churches, because they are generally located in the hardest fields, where churches working on the old lines have utterly failed, many having died and many having run away to save their lives.

A test applied to all the churches of the Congregational denomination showed that during the preceding year the average socialized church had precisely six times as many additions on confession of faith as the average non-institutional church, while all that was accomplished by the former in behalf of cleaner and healthier bodies, better informed minds, and a more wholesome social and civic life was a bonus, over against which the old-line churches had nothing to show.

Robert Woods: THE CITY WILDERNESS

Another man who sought to meet the challenge of the city through the "socialized" or "reconstructive" use of traditional virtues was Robert Woods. In devoting his life to settlement house work in Boston, he tried to redeem the city by creating a vital sense of community in tenement house neighborhoods.

I T IS nowadays almost an axiom that unwise charity only increases the burdens of the poor. It will soon be well understood, also, that scattered good impulses of every sort bring forth "vain works" and "deadly doing."

From Robert Woods, ed., *The City Wilderness: A Settlement Study* (Boston: Houghton Mifflin Company, 1898), pp. 247–259, 273–274.

To see truth clearly, however, is not to see it whole. Even the most discriminating relief-giving has no access to the far-reaching causes of poverty; and, if it set itself up as adequate to the problem of the poor, may even accentuate distress. Philanthropic effort, dealing with a wider range of need, may be able to come more closely at causes; but it is fitful and lacks permanence. There are "philanthropic waves," and often when need is blackest the wave recedes. Sooner or later it will be seen that effort toward social regeneration, like statesmanship, must call out restorative energies which reach as deep as the difficulty and are as lasting in their nature.

Looked at in this way, the agencies for social improvement in the district go into three quite distinct classes. These may be characterized under the analogy of the treatment of sickness. During the acute stage of disease there must be specific remedies of an artificial kind. When this stage is passed there is need, for the time being, of some unusual and specially favoring natural conditions, such as rest or change of scene. Finally, and above all, there must be a radical reorganization of habits, through which the patient, relying upon such means as are continuously accessible to him, shall establish for himself a healthier order of life.

Charity work of all kinds, centering its attention upon the relief of rudimentary human distress as it arises, has from the social point of view a *remedial* effect.

Philanthropic agencies, presupposing the supply of bare bodily wants and providing some of the distinctive means of happy and noble existence, drawing their chief resources from without the life of the district, may be said to serve the valuable *recuperative* function in the cure of social ills.

The really vital policy — within the lines of local action — is the one which aims to build up a better life for the district out of its own material and by means of its own reserve of vitality. In so far as its social undertakings embody this principle, they have the enduring *reconstructive* quality.

The problem of poor-relief throughout the district is divided between the Overseers of the Poor and the Associated Charities. It is understood between the City officials and the private organization that they shall, as far as possible, have separate fields. The Overseers look out for families frequently or chronically in distress, including the half-pauperized, — those whose only gleam of pride in the matter of demanding aid comes from the consideration that some relative has paid taxes, and they therefore are really entitled to a dividend from the City. The Associated Charities take care of those who have not yet made the habit of dependence.

The Overseers, as far as possible, make their clients work for what they receive. Men living at home are required to saw wood for food supplied their families. Homeless men and women are given shelter and food in return for work at the Wayfarers' Lodge and the Women's Shelter, both at the other end of the city. The more extreme cases of pauperism find their way to the City almshouse on Long Island in Boston Harbor.

Poor people who fall into occasional and temporary distress, and may be kept from becoming chronic charity patients, are dealt with in the more quiet and sympathetic way of the Associated Charities. Three separate committees or "conferences" divide the district among them. The work of each is in the hands of a group of volunteer visitors with a woman agent as paid executive. There are weekly meetings, and the office of each conference is open on certain hours every day but Sunday. In addition to dealing with cases of distress as they arise, the conferences act as a sort of local council charged with the entire charity problem of their respective territories. In the main the visitors come from other parts of the city, but church missionaries and residents of settlements if not members of conferences are at least in constant relations with them. One of the best achievements of the Associated Charities has been in the way of allaying rivalries of different kinds, so far as they affect the relief of the poor.

The Associated Charities supply a registration office and clearing-house, covering, so far as possible, all applicants for alms in the city, and all sources of supply. Technically this organization does not itself give material aid. For this it relies largely upon the old charities of Boston, such as the Provident Association and the Howard Benevolent Society; though of course its own visitors, acting as individuals, often secure what is needed in particular cases.

Many of the wise restraints upon thoughtless giving, to which the Associated Charities for long bore solitary witness, have now been generally adopted throughout the district. Relief-giving by church visitors has taken on this more intelligent character. St. Stephen's Church has a weekly conference of its staff for the consideration of cases of distress. The chapters of the Society of St. Vincent de Paul at the Catholic churches also have meetings every week of their visitors among the poor.

Not unfrequently cases are still found of people who maintain a course of pauperism by systematically securing aid from a variety of sources; but the family records of the Associated Charities, now covering a period of twenty years, more

and more effectually prevent this. Begging is comparatively rare in the district. Asking for alms on the streets is forbidden by City ordinance. It is now confined almost wholly to a few pseudo-musicians, whose need is often commensurate with their service, and a varying number of men asking at night for the price of a lodging.

The special task of child-saving is in the hands of two societies which, like all the general charities, have their headquarters in the northern part of the city. The Children's Aid Society, a very progressive and efficient organization, devotes itself in a variety of ways to children who are destitute, neglected or wayward, caring both for those remaining at home and for those who are boarded out. The Society for the Prevention of Cruelty to Children takes legal measures for rescuing abused children, whom it ordinarily turns over to the public authorities. The municipal department for the care of children is now in charge of an able unpaid commission, which is fast taking the City's juvenile wards out of institutions and placing them with country families, subject to the constant oversight of the board's visitors.

The day nurseries of the district do excellent child-saving service. Along with the most scrupulous care of the children goes a large amount of visiting in the homes out of which the children come. The nurseries are so distributed as to meet the full need of the district so far as it concerns hard-working and deserving mothers who have to leave their homes during the day. It is a much-mooted question among nursery workers whether children both of whose parents are unworthy ought to be received into the nurseries, lest to do so should only confirm the parents in their evil ways. It would seem reasonably clear, however, that the interest of the innocent and hopeful child ought to be paramount, and that he should not be neglected for the sake of gaining leverage upon his back-sliding elders.

Considerable effort is made, here and there, to provide work for the unemployed. There are several philanthropic employment bureaus in the district; and the Industrial Aid Society, which covers the city in its scope, has frequent applications from this district. Three local wood-yards give employment to about a hundred men at a time. A temporary home for working women, without any suggestion of reformatory or even of preventive purpose, presents to every woman an escape from the last recourse to which she might be driven.

The degraded element in the community is not despaired of, though the results of effort in this direction are not encouraging. Some interesting temperance propaganda is carried on by reformed men in public meetings conducted by themselves, and an active temperance campaign goes with the work of the various rescue missions. There is not a little earnest endeavor toward the reclamation of women who lead an evil life. Though the personal devotion shown in this cause is beyond praise, it must be said that there is no form of human helpfulness so totally inadequate to the need it aims to meet. There is, indeed, little ground for hope once the awful step is taken. Such rescue homes as are needed have usually been placed outside of this district, some of them in the suburbs, thus taking their protégées away from the region where their chief temptations lie.

The outline of charitable effort within our boundaries should perhaps include passing reference to several institutions, — the Children's Mission for orphans and waifs, on Tremont Street near the business part of the city; the Working Boys' Home, under Roman Catholic auspices, on Bennet Street; the Boston Female Asylum for destitute girls, opposite the Wells Memorial Institute on Washington Street, the oldest charity in this part of the city; and the Washingtonian Home, an inebriate asylum, on Waltham Street, a relic of the old temperance societies of that name. All of these accomplish useful results, but they have litle direct bearing upon the life of the district.

The most searching charity is that which, after relieving acute distress, proceeds to introduce unusual helpful influences in order to ward off the immediate recurrence of the trouble. Such a motive leads at once into those activities which, taken in their relation to social progress, have been described as recuperative. This kind of work has a profound deterrent value; but the great positive use and the absorbing human interest which it has in itself make that consideration merely incidental. The chief reliance in such effort is upon informal friendly acquaintance. This sort of approach, if it be unaffected, has no limits to its efficacy; but naturally it touches first that which is most accessible and most easily influenced, the life of the child. This is the reason why, as philanthropy has developed, the boys' or girls' club has come to be almost as well recognized an institution in the South End as the public school itself.

The two most important centers for boys' and girls' clubs, judging by the quality of the performance as well as by other tests, are the Ellis Memorial Club and Lincoln House. The career of both has been of unusual interest. The Lincoln Club came into existence in 1887 in a very small way, under the initiative of two young women who are still at the head of the enlarged enterprise. The Ellis

Memorial Club had a similar and a still earlier origin. The Ellis building contains a gymnasium, ample meeting rooms, and some sleeping quarters for boys who may be temporarily or permanently without a home. It is located at a point about midway between the homes of the club directors, mostly women, in the Back Bay, and the homes of the rank and file of the members, in the South Cove. No club in Boston deals with boys that have more adverse conditions to meet. The close generous relations that exist between the directors and the boys — year after year until boys become men — has been the means of saving a number of the members from an evil course of life before they had entered upon it, or when they had gone but a little way. Some regularly conducted classes are held, and there is a well used library and a small gymnasium; but the exercises are in the main of a friendly, informal nature. The great object is to secure an influence that will deeply affect the character of the boys. The continued devotion and enthusiasm of the corps of workers, all of whom are volunteers, in a marked way achieves this result. There are now three weekly gatherings, one for girls, one for small boys, and one for youths of sixteen and upwards. During the year there are parties and entertainments to which the families of members come.

At Lincoln House, where in addition to a considerable volunteer force there is a salaried staff, the scheme of club organization is very comprehensive, and there is systematic manual and athletic training. Here, as also at Ellis Memorial, many members of the young men's club have been the boys of the boys' club from year to year in the past. In both cases there is a distinct club spirit, one might almost say a club type. At Lincoln House constant effort is made to relate the club life to the family life of the members and to the positive interests of the local district. There is a degree of sturdy progressiveness about the young men's club. It has hotly contested debates with the Ellis Memorial Club, athletic exhibitions, and dramatic shows. There is nothing in the city so delightful in their way as the dancing parties, given by the young men and women of Lincoln House.

A small organization called the Jefferson Club ought to be mentioned for the interest attaching to its origin as well as for the spirit that has gone into it. This club was founded four years ago by a group of Harvard men, then undergraduates, and has been carried on continuously by Harvard students under leadership transferred from class to class. The Barnard Memorial has always extended its hospitality to this form of work for boys. For long the Lincoln Club met here. Another club under skilled leadership, having now about fifty members, was formed when the Lincoln Club removed to its new building. A unique form of club is that conducted by the Children's Aid Society in various parts of the city under the name "home libraries." There are seven of these in this district. The nucleus of interest is a library of twenty books, — replaced in due season by different ones, — which is kept in some tenement-house home. Once a week some young man or woman, as regular leader, meets the members of each library — usually boys and girls together. The members number eight or ten and live in or near the house in which the books are kept. At the meetings books are exchanged and discussed, and the leader finds a natural means of influence in such conversation and amusements as may follow.

The establishment in this district half a dozen years ago of the two first college settlements in Boston — the South End House, for men, and Denison House, for women — had a distinct influence upon club work for boys and girls. The settlement clubs, as such, do not stand as models of organization; they represent, rather, an important means by which a new moral relation is set up in the ordinary round of neighborhood life. The cardinal points of the settlement policy with regard to the clubs are: that the groups should be small; that the leaders should be "lavish of personal influence;" that, whatever intellectual result may be gained, the really vital thing is to soften and moralize the child in his inner life; that boys and girls should often be brought together in relations of mutual respect and consideration; that the watchword "save the children" is comparatively empty unless that bad home environment is dealt with which so engraves itself upon the soul when it is "wax to receive and marble to retain."

* * *

The settlements reach across the line of distinction . . . between all sorts of charitable and philanthropic work on the one hand and effort directed toward social reconstruction on the other. It is this thoroughgoing reconstructive motive, taking deep hold upon the district's own organized life, depending largely if not entirely upon its inherent resources, that gives the most solid promise of lasting future results. There is not only a constant tendency for philanthropy to widen

its range — it tends to evolve into something higher. As to the settlements in particular, it cannot be too decisively stated that philanthropy, however well devised, is not their final end and aim. Their real use in the world is to reestablish on a natural basis those social relations which modern city life has thrown into confusion, and to develop such new form of cooperative and public action as the changed situation may demand. To foster and sustain the home under tenement conditions, to rehabilitate neighborhood life and give it some of that healthy corporate vitality which a well-ordered village has; to undertake objective investigation of local conditions; to aid organized labor both in the way of inculcating higher aims and in the way of supporting its just demands; to furnish a neutral ground where separated classes, rich and poor, professional and industrial, capitalist and wage-earning, may meet each other on the basis of common humanity; to initiate local cooperation for substantial good purposes; to strive for a better type of local politics and to take part in municipal affairs as they affect the district; to secure for the district its full share of all the best fruits of the city's intellectual and moral progress; to lead people throughout the city to join with them in their aim and motive — this is what the settlements understand to be their vocation; this is the kind of influence which they are silently, year by year, instilling into the inner currents of the district's life.

Jane Addams: THE SPIRIT OF YOUTH AND THE CITY STREETS

In 1889, with Ellen Gates Starr, Jane Addams founded Hull-House in Chicago. This settlement house, patterned after Toynbee Hall in London, became a social center for the underprivileged. Through her many books and essays and her active support of reform movements, Miss Addams, like Robert Woods, hoped to create in urban America the moral equivalent of a rural sense of community. The following chapter from The Spirit of Youth and the City Streets *expresses her point of view in rather unsophisticated terms.*

NOTHING is more certain than that each generation longs for a reassurance as to the value and charm of life, and is secretly afraid lest it lose its sense of the youth of the earth. This is doubtless one reason why it so passionately cherishes its poets and artists who have been able to explore for themselves and to reveal to others the perpetual springs of life's self-renewal.

And yet the average man cannot obtain this desired reassurance through literature nor yet through glimpses of earth and sky. It can come to him only through the chance embodiment of joy and youth which life itself may throw in his way. It is doubtless true that for the mass of men the message is never so unchallenged and so invincible as when embodied in youth itself. One generation after another has depended upon its young to equip it with gaiety and enthusiasm, to persuade it that living is a pleasure, until men everywhere have anxiously provided channels through which this wine of life might flow, and be preserved for their delight. The classical city promoted play with careful solicitude, building the theater and stadium as it built the market place and the temple. The Greeks held their games so integral a part of religion and patriotism that they came to expect from their poets the highest utterances at the very moments when the sense of pleasure released the national life. In the medieval city the knights held their tourneys, the guilds their pageants, the people their dances, and the church made festival for its most cherished saints with gay street processions, and presented a drama in which no less a theme than the history of creation became a matter of thrilling interest. Only in the modern city have men concluded that it is no longer necessary for the municipality to provide for the insatiable desire for play. In so far as they have acted upon this conclusion, they have entered upon a most difficult and dangerous experiment; and this at the very moment when the city has become distinctly industrial, and daily labor is continually more monotonous and subdivided. We forget how new the modern city is, and how short the span of time in which we have assumed that we can eliminate public provision for recreation.

A further difficulty lies in the fact that this industrialism has gathered together multitudes of eager young creatures from all quarters of the earth as a labor supply for the countless factories and workshops, upon which the present industrial city is based. Never before in civilization have

From Jane Addams, *The Spirit of Youth and the City Streets* (New York: The Macmillan Company, 1926), pp. 3–21. Reprinted by permission of Myra Reynolds Linn and John A. Brittain.

such numbers of young girls been suddenly released from the protection of the home and permitted to walk unattended upon city streets and to work under alien roofs; for the first time they are being prized more for their labor power than for their innocence, their tender beauty, their ephemeral gaiety. Society cares more for the products they manufacture than for their immemorial ability to reaffirm the charm of existence. Never before have such numbers of young boys earned money independently of the family life, and felt themselves free to spend it as they choose in the midst of vice deliberately disguised as pleasure.

This stupid experiment of organizing work and failing to organize play has, of course, brought about a fine revenge. The love of pleasure will not be denied, and when it has turned into all sorts of malignant and vicious appetites, then we, the middle aged, grow quite distracted and resort to all sorts of restrictive measures. We even try to dam up the sweet fountain itself because we are affrighted by these neglected streams; but almost worse than the restrictive measures is our apparent belief that the city itself has no obligation in the matter, an assumption upon which the modern city turns over to commercialism practically all the provisions for public recreation.

Quite as one set of men has organized the young people into industrial enterprises in order to profit from their toil, so another set of men and also of women, I am sorry to say, have entered the neglected field of recreation and have organized enterprises which make profit out of this invincible love of pleasure.

In every city arise so-called "places" — "gin-palaces," they are called in fiction; in Chicago we euphemistically say merely "places," — in which alcohol is dispensed, not to allay thirst, but, ostensibly to stimulate gaiety, it is sold really in order

to empty pockets. Huge dance halls are opened to which hundreds of young people are attracted, many of whom stand wistfully outside a roped circle, for it requires five cents to procure within it for five minutes the sense of allurement and intoxication which is sold in lieu of innocent pleasure. These coarse and illicit merrymakings remind one of the unrestrained jollities of Restoration London, and they are indeed their direct descendants, properly commercialized, still confusing joy with lust, and gaiety with debauchery. Since the soldiers of Cromwell shut up the people's playhouses and destroyed their pleasure fields, the Anglo-Saxon city has turned over the provision for public recreation to the most evil-minded and the most unscrupulous members of the community. We see thousands of girls walking up and down the streets on a pleasant evening with no chance to catch a sight of pleasure even through a lighted window, save as these lurid places provide it. Apparently the modern city sees in these girls only two possibilities, both of them commercial: first, a chance to utilize by day their new and tender labor power in its factories and shops, and then another chance in the evening to extract from them their petty wages by pandering to their love of pleasure.

As these overworked girls stream along the street, the rest of us see only the self-conscious walk, the giggling speech, the preposterous clothing. And yet through the huge hat, with its wilderness of bedraggled feathers, the girl announces to the world that she is here. She demands attention to the fact of her existence, she states that she is ready to live, to take her place in the world. The most precious moment in human development is the young creature's assertion that he is unlike any other human being, and has an individual contribution to make to the world. The variation from the established type is at the root of all change, the only possible basis for progress, all that keeps life from growing unprofitably stale and repetitious.

Is it only the artists who really see these young creatures as they are — the artists who are themselves endowed with immortal youth? Is it our disregard of the artist's message which makes us so blind and so stupid, or are we so under the influence of our *Zeitgeist* that we can detect only commercial values in the young as well as in the old? It is as if our eyes were holden to the mystic beauty, the redemptive joy, the civic pride which these multitudes of young people might supply to our dingy towns.

The young creatures themselves piteously look all about them in order to find an adequate means of expression for their most precious message: One day a serious young man came to Hull-House with his pretty young sister who, he explained, wanted to go somewhere every single evening, "although she could only give the flimsy excuse that the flat was too little and too stuffy to stay in." In the difficult rôle of elder brother, he had done his best, stating that he had taken her "to all the missions in the neighborhood, that she had had a chance to listen to some awful good sermons and to some elegant hymns, but that some way she did not seem to care for the society of the best Christian people." The little sister reddened painfully under this cruel indictment and could offer no word of excuse, but a curious thing happened to me. Perhaps it was the phrase "the best Christian people," perhaps it was the delicate color of her flushing cheeks and her swimming eyes, but certain it is, that instantly and vividly there appeared to my mind the delicately tinted piece of wall in a Roman catacomb where the early Christians, through a dozen devices of spring flowers, skipping lambs and a

shepherd tenderly guiding the young, had indelibly written down that the Christian message is one of inexpressible joy. Who is responsible for forgetting this message delivered by the "best Christian people" two thousand years ago? Who is to blame that the lambs, the little ewe lambs, have been so caught upon the brambles?

But quite as the modern city wastes this most valuable moment in the life of the girl, and drives into all sorts of absurd and obscure expressions her love and yearning towards the world in which she forecasts her destiny, so it often drives the boy into gambling and drinking in order to find his adventure.

Of Lincoln's enlistment of two and a half million soldiers, a very large number were under twenty-one, some of them under eighteen, and still others were mere children under fifteen. Even in those stirring times when patriotism and high resolve were at the flood, no one responded as did "the boys," and the great soul who yearned over them, who refused to shoot the sentinels who slept the sleep of childhood, knew, as no one else knew, the precious glowing stuff of which his army was made. But what of the millions of boys who are now searching for adventurous action, longing to fulfil the same high purpose?

One of the most pathetic sights in the public dance halls of Chicago is the number of young men, obviously honest young fellows from the country, who stand about vainly hoping to make the acquaintance of some "nice girl." They look eagerly up and down the rows of girls, many of whom are drawn to the hall by the same keen desire for pleasure and social intercourse which the lonely young men themselves feel.

One Sunday night at twelve o'clock I had occasion to go into a large public dance hall. As I was standing by the rail looking for the girl I had come to find, a young man approached me and quite simply asked me to introduce him to some "nice girl," saying that he did not know any one there. On my replying that a public dance hall was not the best place in which to look for a nice girl, he said: "But I don't know any other place where there is a chance to meet any kind of a girl. I'm awfully lonesome since I came to Chicago." And then he added rather defiantly: "Some nice girls do come here! It's one of the best halls in town." He was voicing the "bitter loneliness" that many city men remember to have experienced during the first years after they had "come up to town." Occasionally the right sort of man and girl meet each other in these dance halls and the romance with such a tawdry beginning ends happily and respectably. But, unfortunately, mingled with the respectable young men seeking to form the acquaintance of young women through the only channel which is available to them, are many young fellows of evil purpose, and among the girls who have left their lonely boarding houses or rigid homes for a "little fling" are likewise women who openly desire to make money from the young men whom they meet, and back of it all is the desire to profit by the sale of intoxicating and "doctored" drinks.

Perhaps never before have the pleasures of the young and mature become so definitely separated as in the modern city. The public dance halls filled with frivolous and irresponsible young people in a feverish search for pleasure, are but a sorry substitute for the old dances on the village green in which all of the older people of the village participated. Chaperonage was not then a social duty but natural and inevitable, and the whole courtship period was guarded by the conventions and restraint which were taken as a matter of course and had developed through years of publicity and simple propriety.

The only marvel is that the stupid attempt to put the fine old wine of traditional country life into the new bottles of the modern town does not lead to disaster oftener than it does, and that the wine so long remains pure and sparkling.

We cannot afford to be ungenerous to the city in which we live without suffering the penalty which lack of fair interpretation always entails. Let us know the modern city in its weakness and wickedness, and then seek to rectify and purify it until it shall be free at least from the grosser temptations which now beset the young people who are living in its tenement houses and working in its factories. The mass of these young people are possessed of good intentions and they are equipped with a certain understanding of city life. This itself could be made a most valuable social instrument toward securing innocent recreation and better social organization. They are already serving the city in so far as it is honeycombed with mutual benefit societies, with "pleasure clubs," with organizations connected with churches and factories which are filling a genuine social need. And yet the whole apparatus for supplying pleasure is wretchedly inadequate and full of danger to whomsoever may approach it. Who is responsible for its inadequacy and dangers? We certainly cannot expect the fathers and mothers who have come to the city from farms or who have emigrated from other lands to appreciate or rectify these dangers. We cannot expect the young people themselves to cling to conventions which are totally unsuited to modern city conditions, nor yet to be equal to the task of forming new conventions through which this more agglomerate social life may express itself. Above all we cannot hope that they will understand the emotional force which seizes them and which, when it does not find the traditional line of domesticity, serves as a cancer in the very tissues of society and as a disrupter of the securest social bonds. No attempt is made to treat the manifestations of this fundamental instinct with dignity or to give it possible social utility. The spontaneous joy, the clamor for pleasure, the desire of the young people to appear finer and better and altogether more lovely than they really are, the idealization not only of each other but of the whole earth which they regard but as a theater for their noble exploits, the unworldly ambitions, the romantic hopes, the make-believe world in which they live, if properly utilized, what might they not do to make our sordid cities more beautiful, more companionable? And yet at the present moment every city is full of young people who are utterly bewildered and uninstructed in regard to the basic experience which must inevitably come to them, and which has varied, remote, and indirect expressions.

Even those who may not agree with the authorities who claim that it is this fundamental sex susceptibility which suffuses the world with its deepest meaning and beauty, and furnishes the momentum towards all art, will perhaps permit me to quote the classical expression of this view as set forth in that ancient and wonderful conversation between Socrates and the wise woman Diotima. Socrates asks: "What are they doing who show all this eagerness and heat which is called love? And what is the object they have in view? Answer me." Diotima replies: "I will teach you. The object which they have in view is birth in beauty, whether of body or soul. . . . For love, Socrates, is not as you imagine the love of the beautiful only . . . . but the love of birth in beauty, because to the mortal creature generation is a sort of eternity and immortality."

To emphasize the eternal aspects of love is not of course an easy undertaking, even if we follow the clue afforded by the heart of every generous lover. His experience at least in certain moments tends to pull him on and out from the passion for one to an enthusiasm for that highest beauty and excellence of which the most perfect form is but an inadequate expression. Even the most loutish tenement-house youth vaguely feels this, and at least at rare intervals reveals it in his talk to his "girl." His memory unexpectedly brings hidden treasures to the surface of consciousness and he recalls the more delicate and tender experiences of his childhood and earlier youth. "I remember the time when my little sister died, that I rode out to the cemetery feeling that everybody in Chicago had moved away from the town to make room for that kid's funeral, everything was so darned lonesome and yet it was kind of peaceful too." Or, "I never had a chance to go into the country when I was a kid, but I remember one day when I had to deliver a package way out on the West Side, that I saw a flock of sheep in Douglas Park. I had never thought that a sheep could be anywhere but in a picture, and when I saw those big white spots on the green grass beginning to move and to turn into sheep, I felt exactly as if Saint Cecilia had come out of her frame over the organ and was walking in the park." Such moments come into the life of the most prosaic youth living in the most crowded quarters of the cities. What do we do to encourage and to solidify those moments, to make them come true in our dingy towns, to give them expression in forms of art?

We not only fail in this undertaking but even debase existing forms of art. We are informed by high authority that there is nothing in the environment to which youth so keenly responds as to music, and yet the streets, the vaudeville shows, the five-cent theaters are full of the most blatant and vulgar songs. The trivial and obscene words, the meaningless and flippant airs run through the heads of hundreds of young people for hours at a time while they are engaged in monotonous factory work. We totally ignore that ancient connection between music and morals which was so long insisted upon by philosophers as well as poets. The street music has quite broken away from all control, both of the educator and the patriot, and we have grown singularly careless in regard to its influence upon young people. Although we legislate against it in saloons because of its dangerous influence there, we constantly permit music on the street to incite that which should be controlled, to degrade that which should be exalted, to make sensuous that which might be lifted into the realm of the higher imagination.

Our attitude towards music is typical of our carelessness towards all those things which make for common joy and for the restraints of high civilization on the streets. It is as if our cities had not yet developed a sense of responsibility in regard to the life of the streets, and continually forget that recreation is stronger than vice, and that recreation alone can stifle the lust for vice.

Perhaps we need to take a page from the philosophy of the Greeks to whom the world of fact was also the world of the ideal, and to whom the realization of what ought to be, involved not the destruction of what was, but merely its perfecting upon its own lines. To the Greeks virtue was not a hard conformity to a law felt as alien to the natural character, but a free expression of the inner life. To treat thus the fundamental susceptibility of sex which now so bewilders the street life and drives young people themselves into all sorts of difficulties, would mean to loosen it from the things of sense and to link it to the affairs of the imagination. It would mean to fit to this gross and heavy stuff the wings of the mind, to scatter from it "the clinging mud of banality and vulgarity," and to speed it on through our city streets amid spontaneous laughter, snatches of lyric song, the recovered forms of old dances, and the traditional rondels of merry games. It would thus bring charm and beauty to the prosaic city and connect it subtly with the arts of the past as well as with the vigor and renewed life of the future.

III. THE HOPE OF THE CITY

William Dean Howells: THE WHITE CITY OF THE FUTURE

William Dean Howells, one of America's finest novelists and literary critics, wrote two novels describing life on the imaginary continent of Altruria — his vision of utopia. In the selection below from A Traveler from Altruria, *Aristedes Homos, the traveler, compares Altruria's ideal "capitals" with the fallen cities they replaced. In the second selection, from the sequel,* Through the Eye of the Needle, *Mr. Homos' new wife, an American, writes letters describing Altruria to a friend back in the United States.*

ALTRURIA

WE HAD, of course, a great many large cities under the old egoistic conditions, which increased and fattened upon the country, and fed their cancerous life with fresh infusions of its blood. We had several cities of half a million, and one of more than a million; we had a score of them with a population of a hundred thousand or more. We were very proud of them, and vaunted them as a proof of our unparalleled prosperity, though really they never were anything but congeries of millionaires and the wretched creatures who served them and supplied them. Of course, there was everywhere the appearance of enterprise and activity, but it meant final loss for the great mass of the business men, large and small, and final gain for the millionaires. These and their parasites dwelt together, the rich starving the poor and the poor plundering and misgoverning the rich; and it was the intolerable suffering in the cities that chiefly hastened the fall of the old Accumulation, and the rise of the Commonwealth.

Almost from the moment of the Evolution the competitive and monopolistic centers of population began to decline. In the clear light of the new order it was seen that they were not fit dwelling-places for men, either in the complicated and luxurious palaces where the rich fenced themselves from their kind, or in the vast tenements, towering height upon height, ten and twelve stories up, where the swarming poor festered in vice and sickness and famine. If I were to tell you of the fashion of those cities of our egoistic epoch, how the construction was one error from the first, and every correction of an error bred a new defect, I should make you laugh, I should make you weep. We let them fall to ruin as quickly as they would, and their sites are still so pestilential, after the lapse of centuries, that travellers are publicly guarded against them. Ravening beasts and poisonous reptiles lurk in those abodes of the riches and the poverty that are no longer known to our life. A part of one of the less malarial of the old cities, however, is maintained by the commonwealth in the form of its prosperity, and is studied by antiquarians for the instruction, and by moralists for the admonition it affords.

From William Dean Howells, *A Traveler from Altruria* (New York: Harper and Brothers, 1894), pp. 281–285.

A section of a street is exposed, and you see the foundations of the houses; you see the filthy drains that belched into the common sewers, trapped and retrapped to keep the poison gases down; you see the sewers that rolled their loathsome tides under the streets, amidst a tangle of gas pipes, steam pipes, water pipes, telegraph wires, electric lighting wires, electric motor wires and grip-cables; all without a plan, but make-shifts, expedients, devices, to repair and evade the fundamental mistake of having any such cities at all.

There are now no cities in Altruria, in your meaning, but there are capitals, one for each of the Regions of our country, and one for the whole commonwealth. These capitals are for the transaction of public affairs, in which every citizen of Altruria is schooled, and they are the residences of the administrative officials, who are alternated every year, from the highest to the lowest. A public employment with us is of no greater honor or profit than any other, for with our absolute economic equality, there can be no ambition, and there is no opportunity for one citizen to outshine another. But as the capitals are the centers of all the arts, which we consider the chief of our public affairs, they are oftenest frequented by poets, actors, painters, sculptors, musicians and architects. We regard all artists, who are in a sort creators, as the human type which is likest the divine, and we try to conform our whole industrial life to the artistic temperament. Even in the labors of the field and shop, which are obligatory upon all, we study the inspirations of this temperament, and in the voluntary pursuits we allow it full control. Each, in these, follows his fancy as to what he shall do, and when he shall

do it, or whether he shall do anything at all. In the capitals are the universities, theaters, galleries, museums, cathedrals, laboratories and conservatories, and the appliances of every art and science, as well as the administration buildings; and beauty as well as use is studied in every edifice. Our capitals are as clean and quiet and healthful as the country, and these advantages are secured simply by the elimination of the horse, an animal which we should be as much surprised to find in the streets of a town as the plesiosaurus or the pterodactyl. All transportation in the capitals, whether for pleasure or business, is by electricity, and swift electrical expresses connect the capital of each region with the villages which radiate from it to the cardinal points. These expresses run at the rate of a hundred and fifty miles an hour, and they enable the artist, the scientist, the literary man, of the remotest hamlet, to visit the capital (when he is not actually resident there in some public use) every day, after the hours of the obligatory industries; or if he likes, he may remain there a whole week or fortnight, giving six hours a day instead of three to the obligatories, until the time is made up. In case of very evident merit, or for the purpose of allowing him to complete some work requiring continuous application, a vote of the local agents may release him from the obligatories indefinitely. Generally, however, our artists prefer not to ask this, but avail themselves of the stated means we have of allowing them to work at the obligatories, and get the needed exercise and variety of occupation, in the immediate vicinity of the capital.

❁   ❁   ❁

I SUPPOSE you are anxious, if these letters which are piling up and piling up should ever reach you, or even start to do so, to know something about the Altrurian cities, and what they are like. Well, in the first place, you must cast all images of American cities out of your mind, or any European cities, except, perhaps, the prettiest and stateliest parts of Paris, where there is a regular sky-line, and the public buildings and monuments are approached through shaded avenues. There are no private houses here, in our sense — that is, houses which people have built with their own money on their own land, and made as ugly outside and as molestive to their neighbors and the passers-by as they chose. As the buildings belong to the whole people, the first requirement is that they shall be beautiful inside and out. There are a few grand edifices looking like Greek temples, which are used for the government offices, and these are, of course, the most dignified, but the dwellings are quite as attractive and comfortable. They are built round courts, with gardens and flowers in the courts, and wide grassy spaces round them. They are rather tall, but never so tall as our great hotels or apartment-houses, and the floors are brought to one level by elevators, which are used only in the capitals; and, generally speaking, I should say the villages were pleasanter than the cities. In fact, the village is the Altrurian ideal, and there is an effort everywhere to reduce the size of the towns and increase the number of the villages. The outlying farms have been gathered into these, and now there is not one of those lonely places in the country, like those where our farmers toil alone outdoors and their wives alone indoors, and both go mad so often in the solitude. The villages are almost in sight of each other, and the people go to their fields in company, while the women carry on their housekeeping cooperatively, with a large kitchen which they use in common; they have their meals apart or together, as they like. If any one is sick or disabled the neighbors come in and help do her work, as they used with us in the early times, and as they still do in country places. Village life here is preferred, just as country life is in England, and one thing that will amuse you, with your American ideas, and your pride in the overgrowth of our cities: the Altrurian papers solemnly announce from time to time that the population of such or such a capital has been reduced so many hundreds or thousands since the last census. That means that the villages in the neighborhood have been increased in number and population.

Meanwhile, I must say the capitals are delightful: clean, airy, quiet, with the most beautiful architecture, mostly classic and mostly marble, with rivers running through them and round them, and every real convenience, but not a clutter of artificial conveniences, as with us. In the streets there are noiseless trolleys (where they have not been replaced by public automobiles) which the long distances of the ample ground-plan make rather necessary, and the rivers are shot over with swift motor-boats; for the short distances you always expect to walk, or if you don't expect it, you walk anyway. The car-lines and boat-lines are public, and they are free, for the Altrurians think that the

From William Dean Howells, *Through the Eye of the Needle* (New York: Harper and Brothers, 1907), pp. 178–180, 184–185. Printed by permission of W. W. Howells.

community owes transportation to every one who lives beyond easy reach of the points which their work calls them to.

* * *

I despair of giving you any *real* notion of the capitals, but if you remember the White City at the Columbian Fair at Chicago in 1893, you can have some idea of the general effect of one; only there is nothing heterogeneous in their beauty. There is one classic rule in the architecture, but each of the different architects may characterize an edifice from himself, just as different authors writing the same language characterize it by the diction natural to him. There are suggestions of the capitals in some of our cities, and if you remember Commonwealth Avenue in Boston, you can imagine something like the union of street and garden which every street of them is. The trolleys run under the overarching trees between the lawns, flanked by gravelled footpaths between flower-beds, and you take the cars or not as you like. As there is no hurry, they go about as fast as English trams, and the danger from them is practically reduced to nothing by the crossings dipping under them at the street corners. The centre of the capital is approached by colonnades, which at night bear groups of great bulbous lamps, and by day flutter with the Altrurian and Regionic flags. Around this centre are the stores and restaurants and theatres, and galleries and libraries, with arcades over the sidewalks, like those in Bologna; sometimes the arcades are in two stories, as they are in Chester. People are constantly coming and going in an easy way during the afternoon, though in the morning the streets are rather deserted.

But what is the use? I could go on describing and describing, and never get in half the differences from American cities, with their hideous uproar, and their mud in the wet, and their clouds of swirling dust in the wind. But there is one feature which I must mention, because you can fancy it from the fond dream of a great national highway which some of our architects projected while they were still in the fervor of excitement from the beauty of the Peristyle, and other features of the White City. They really have such a highway here, crossing the whole Altrurian continent, and uniting the circle of the Regionic capitals. As we travelled for a long time by the country roads on the beds of the old railways, I had no idea of this magnificent avenue, till one day my husband suddenly ran our van into the one leading up to the first capital we were to visit. Then I found myself between miles and miles of stately white pillars, rising and sinking as the road found its natural levels, and growing in the perspective before us and dwindling behind us. I could not keep out of my mind a colonnade of palm-trees, only the fronds were lacking, and there were never palms so beautiful.

Dana Bartlett: THE BETTER CITY

*Dana Bartlett was a social worker in Los Angeles and Director of the
Bethlehem Institutions, a non-sectarian institutional church. His views
of improving the city, however, were much less parochial than those
of many social workers, because he was able to see hope in the city
itself, as well as in traditional virtues. This passage from his book,* The
Better City, *explains his optimism about Los Angeles in terms of the
climate and the strides then being taken to improve living conditions
and encourage city beautification.*

A GREAT city is forming by the shore
of the sunset sea. Great and still
greater will it become as the years go by,
until it stretches itself from the Sierra
Madre Mountains to the Pacific.

* * *

With this fair land for its setting, the
City Beautiful of which we are to speak
is to be built up. The story of its gradual
enlargement must be told at length in another chapter. We shall now seek to indicate some of the reasons why we expect
this to be a greater and a better city.

In the first place, there is the asset of
climate, and there is no climate on earth
equal to this, for it is enjoyable and
health-giving the year around. When
elsewhere men are suffering from the
heat, in this favored clime the least shade
is always cooling and blankets are necessary for comfort at night. When in the
North and East the mercury goes down
below zero, and the rivers are frozen over
and the land is covered with snow, in
this city men sleep with open windows,
or live comfortably either in a tent house
or out of doors, save in the rainy season.
Here homes are built with reference to
the climate, with large porches used as
living rooms, with open-air bedrooms,
with patios filled with blossom and rare

plants — the joy of every season. Within
a few miles of this city are to be found
the beaches that furnish a climate cool
in summer and wonderfully pleasant in
winter. The mountains are near by, always enticing and invigorating, and in
the winter furnish the touch of snow for
those who desire the chill, so that they
may experience again the crisp air of
their old home winter. Thousands of children and youths in this city have never
seen snow nearer than the distant mountain tops, and yet this is not an enervat-
ing climate. It is unlike the tropics,
where because of the excessive moisture
and heat, men are content to sit down
under the bread-fruit tree and live without much labor. Here with the air
charged with electricity and ozone, there
is a bracing quality that makes the sick
well and the strong capable of doing hard
work without great exhaustion.

Climate has a cash value. It is the
climate that brings hither three-fourths
of the tourists, and leads the majority to
stay after they have spent a winter where
none of the rigors of winter weather are
experienced. This is a national play-
ground. The rich from all over the world
are coming hither on pleasure bent.
Nearly every day is a fine day, and life
may be one round of joy. Hither comes

From Dana Bartlett, *The Better City: A Sociological Study of a Modern City* (Los Angeles: The
Neuner Press, 1907), pp. 11, 17–27, 43–44.

not only the invalid, but the man of business that he may find the quiet and peaceful closing of a happy life. A recent writer, enthusiastic, yet keeping well within bounds, says:

Here is the climate of the tropics without its perils; here is the fertility of Egypt without its fellaheen; here are the fruits and flowers of Sicily without its lazzaroni; here the beauty of Italy without its limited market; the sunshine of Persia without its oppressions. For this is America, with its unfettered freedom and unfettered energy.

But to none has the climate such a cash value as to the working man. No days lost because of the storm or cold; no using up in winter of that which has been saved in summer; no suffering from lack of coal or clothing. On the other hand, he is able to possess a home of his own, and though its walls may be only the thickness of a single board, yet covered with flowers and vines, it equals in comfort an Eastern palace. In this clime the rancher sees many of his crops grow continuously, and is able to reap in winter as well as in summer. In such a climate the struggle for existence will always be modified, and can never under the worst conditions be like that of other cities.

This climate has its sociological bearing on the housing problem — for here the tendency is to open and not to crowded quarters; on morality, for those who cultivate a taste for natural pleasures are not tempted to the grosser sins. Here even the pauper lives in surroundings fit for a king. It has its bearing on health. Every sensible doctor will recommend the "open-air cure" as the most effectual remedy for nearly every disease. And here there are more perfect days during the year for out-of-door life, than are to be found anywhere else. Plenty of fresh air with absence of worry, peace of mind and some definite object in life will surely bring health to any of God's creatures.

Another reason why Los Angeles is to be not only a greater but a better city, is found in the fact that it is largely an American city. The majority of its citizens are of American birth; and its foreign-born citizen, catching the American spirit, vies with his neighbor in his devotion to high ideals. The people of culture have come from every point of the compass to make up the present city of nearly 300,000 and to join with the old settlers in planning for a greater city with a million happy citizens. The amalgamation of races is producing a new and splendid type. Here is a people within whose veins runs the red blood of the hardy Northmen. They are possessed of the push and the stir of the great Eastern cities, and have also the romantic and poetic temperament of the Spanish life in which they share, together with the love of nature and of the beautiful that characterized the early settlers. The out-of-door life, the mission residence, the bungalow, are but the outward expression of the inner thought. Here as in no other city, you can hear the song of the siren mingled with the music of mission bells.

The greatness, at least of the City of the Angels, can be prophesied because its commercial prospects are brighter than ever before. With three great transcontinental lines and the coming of the fourth, with a harbor in the making that will cost the Government about $4,000,-000, with mighty steamships carrying the product of a thousand factories to the teeming millions of the Orient, what can stop this city from becoming one of the great commercial centers of the earth? This city has acquired water rights in the high Sierras that will make it possible to bring from the Owens River in a conduit two hundred and fifty miles long, water sufficient for a city of two millions. In a land where water means so much and where it has the power to transform the desert into a garden, who can picture the beauty and greatness of the future City of the Angels, when this gigantic scheme becomes an accomplished fact?

The first city in the Union to light its streets entirely with electricity, Los Angeles is now one of the best lighted cities in all the land. To one standing on the surrounding mountain tops, the city presents a brilliant appearance with numerous high masts carrying groups of lights, and with the many thousand electric globes marking the streets in every direction. With several of the principal streets lighted by clusters of lights on ornamental iron electroliers, the city seems as though prepared for a perpetual fiesta.

It is easy to become enthused as to the possible greatness of a growing city. While the aim of this book is ethical rather than historical, the author describes the Greater Los Angeles with the hope that there may be awakened an equal enthusiasm regarding the Better Los Angeles. Long years ago this city outgrew the cactus-hedged boundaries of the old pueblo, and now the cry is for a city from the mountains to the sea. Even at the present this is more than a dream, for beginning at Altadena in the foothills, there is hardly a break as the traveler descends by trolley through Pasadena — the Queen of the Valley — South Pasadena, Garvanza, Highland Park, and on through the city itself, toward Long Beach. In the seaward direction, the workingmen own thousands of homes. Compton almost touches the last tract laid out by the Long Beach promoter. Going toward the west, Hollywood, Sher-

man and the Soldiers' Home almost reach that wonderful line of beach resorts extending from Playa del Rey to Santa Monica. In view of this wonderful development, the city has already appointed a committee which has reported favorably on a plan for the consolidation of city and county, by constituting nine boroughs, reaching from San Fernando to San Pedro, and from San Gabriel to the ocean front. At a recent election, a narrow strip of land reaching from the city limits to Wilmington and San Pedro was annexed, thus making it possible to reach tide water where Los Angeles can own its own harbor.

At present there are about 780 miles of streets; and there are plans on foot for the building of a poppy-lined boulevard from Pasadena to the city, continuing it to Long Beach in the Pacific Boulevard, and toward the western sea by an extension of the Sunset Boulevard along the foothill section of the Cahuenga Valley. A kite-shaped boulevard is projected toward the east, touching all the towns in both directions to Redlands and Riverside. In view of all this, together with the development of the rapid transit system — a system already far ahead of other cities, it is small wonder that the mind becomes somewhat intoxicated with the sense of evident destiny.

But it is well to remember that the desire for mere wealth and outward greatness has proved the ruin of many a city. The quest for the dollar blinds the eyes to the higher civic ideals. The fact is, that city life had its Dark Age until the beginning, but a few years ago, of the Civic Renaissance. Then came the "ten years' war" against the slum, made necessary by forty years of neglect and lack of civic self-sacrifice. Graft and misrule in the city hall have only recently been met with high business ideals, and the reapplication of the phrase, "a public office, a public trust."

During the past fifteen years the social workers and the public press have gradually evolved a new patriotism. The social conscience of many has been aroused, and a feeling of community obligation and purpose is possessing many who once lived only the life of selfish commercialism. There has been many a signal victory of right ideals in these last few years. Frederick Howe in the Outlook gives a notable example:

In a few years' time the Cleveland Chamber of Commerce has compelled its members to think about the city in a city way, and today its members talk not so much about bank clearances, tonnage, freight rates, and business for their own personal profit; they talk city, street cleaning, health protection, parks, public baths, schools, model tenements, cheap light, heat, and transportation for all the people. The work is not all done yet, and the commercial impulse is keenly alert when its business interests are involved. But the Chamber has got its bent, and it can never become again a mere temple of money makers.

Los Angeles has been lavishly endowed by Nature with all that goes to make up a prosperous city, and commercially its future is secured. But greatness is not necessarily goodness; indeed, it may be its greatest foe. Is it not then an opportune time to lay emphasis on the Better City, setting forth high ideals as to private virtue and honesty, high ideals as to industrial and civic life, so that the better city may be created for the benefit and enjoyment of all the people?

The writer, after many years spent as a social worker in this city, can testify to the great awakening along all social lines today. Everywhere, among rich and poor alike, there seems to be a deep purpose to make this city not alone greater, but pre-eminently "better, wiser, and fairer."

As this is written the Landmarks Club is preparing to rehabilitate the old missions, planted so long ago amid privation and suffering on the part of the padres. Before long the traveler along the rebuilt Camino Real will be able to pause under the arches of the mission, while the brown-robed Franciscan bids him enter; and in the stillness of its cloisters he will be invited to think of those things that are eternal and abiding, and which make for the true greatness of all human life. Visions, dreams, ideals, they also have a part in the making of the Better City.

THE CITY BEAUTIFUL

Ugliness has no commercial or ethical value. The crowded tenement, the rookery, a city's ill-kept streets and yards are not incentives to higher living. On the other hand, it is a fact made clear by years of experience that the fairer the city, the nearer to Nature's heart the people are brought; the more easily they are governed; there is less crime and more of the normal, spiritual, healthful life which is the product of the ripest civilization.

The last half century has seen a rapid development of factory and commercial life. Will it pay large dividends? has been the only question asked in the building of store or mill. The busy strenuous life has left little time for the study of the beautiful. But new times are upon us. The artist and the artisan, the teacher and the merchant, the social dreamer and the social worker, each in his own way, has plans for the City Beautiful. It is a sign of great promise when the daily papers, usually so filled with commercialism, partisan politics, and with the shadier side of life are giving so much attention to the aesthetic and artistic side of a city's development. One of our city papers devotes a page a week to this subject.

* * *

In Los Angeles much has been done in a local way by Ward Improvement Associations. Some years ago, the Eighth Ward Association, in the most congested part of the city, placed the following circular in every home, with excellent results:

Neighbors, let us cooperate that we may have clean streets and sidewalks, front and rear yards beautified, and healthy surroundings for our children. To this end, let us see that the street in front of the residence is kept clean from paper, tins and all kinds of rubbish. Put cans, bones, ashes in a separate receptacle and place out on garbage days. Teach the children never to throw garbage in the street. It is unsightly, and may be unhealthy. Sweep the sidewalks whenever necessary. Report all cases of broken sinks and closets to the health office, provided the owner will not fix them. Let us beautify our yards. In this wonderful climate, where flowers grow so readily, we may have gardens which would be the pride of the rich in the East. Prepare front yards and back yards if possible; fertilize and plant seeds and vines. The association will gladly donate the seeds and cuttings. The growth of potted plants for porches and windows is recommended. Neighbors, let us cooperate.

No scheme for beautifying the city can be complete that does not include a comprehensive plan for a metropolitan park system. We have scarcely begun to plan for the noiseless city, but are content to allow nerve-racking, unnecessary noises. We join the rush as though there was no time for else but business. We wear out before our time. The park offers the opportunity to escape from the noises and associations of the city, and in touch with Nature, to find repose for mind and body.

The parks are the lungs of the city. They are the sanitariums for the people who cannot afford to hie themselves to the country or seaside. They give sunlight and green fields free of cost. They are the civilizers and equalizers for the poor.

Frederic C. Howe: THE CITY — THE HOPE OF DEMOCRACY

Few men of this period had more faith in the prospects of urban life and institutions than municipal reformer and social scientist Frederic C. Howe. In the first of the two selections reproduced here he argues that the city is not a personal or ethical problem — it is an economic problem that must be solved through planning. In the second part he explains his optimism about the twentieth-century city's ability to improve society through its "legalized freedom" and intelligent democratic organization.

Reprinted from "The City as a Socializing Agency" by Frederic C. Howe, *American Journal of Sociology*, Vol. XVII, No. 5 (March, 1912), pp. 590–593, by permission of The University of Chicago Press.

WE HAVE generally assumed that the city problem was a personal one; that it was a problem of men, of charters, of political machinery. We have approached the city as a personal, ethical, political question. Reform has been directed to securing efficient, honest officials. We have thought of the city as an agency of the state, not unlike the county or the town. We have been like a builder who seeks a care-taker rather than an architect; like a business man who neglects his factory in the perfection of a system of bookkeeping. We have thought of men rather than of things. We have had no city program.

The city problem is primarily an economic, not a personal, problem. Our failure to see this is far more costly than the inefficiency and dishonesty about which so much has been written and for the correction of which so much energy has been expended. The basis of the city, like the basis of all life, is physical. The health, comfort, convenience, happiness of the people is intimately bound up with the material side of the city. Much of the poverty is the product of our neglect to control the economic foundations of the community. The houses we live in, the streets we travel over, the air and the sunlight are controlled by the attitude of the city to physical things. So is the distribution of wealth, the cost of living and the vice and crime of the community. All are intimately connected with the way the city is built, with the economic or social rather than the personal, the ethical, the political questions with which we have been absorbed.

Our cities are what they are because we have not thought of the city as a city, of the town as a town, of the rights of everybody as opposed to the rights of anybody. A million men are thinking only of their individual lot lines, of their inviolable right to do as they will with their own, irrespective of its effect on the community. We do not see beyond our own doorsteps, we do not think in city terms, or appreciate that the progress of society has so far socialized old conditions that the community must have a life of its own separate from, or the composite of, the lives and property of all of its people. We have exalted the rights of the individual above the common weal. Our cities have been permitted to grow with no concern for the future and with no thought of the community or the terrible costs which this uncontrolled development creates.

This failure to think in community terms, to appreciate that the city is a physical thing involves costs which the future cannot repair. And the most costly blunder of all is our neglect of the city's foundations, of the land on which the city is built. The American city is inconvenient, dirty, lacking in charm and beauty because the individual land owner has been permitted to plan it, to build, to do as he willed with his land. There has been no community control, no sense of the public as opposed to private rights.

Our cities have been planned by a hundred different land owners, each desirous of securing the quickest possible speculative returns from the sale of his property. Streets have been laid out without regard to the needs of the future. They have been cheaply paved, watered, and sewered. There have been few building restrictions, little provision for parks, open spaces or sites for public buildings.

The site of a city and the suburbs should be studied with the care of an architect selecting the site of a public building. Streets are worthy of as much thought as a cathedral, which is to endure for centuries. They should be planned with a far-sighted vision of the future. Every bit of land should be allotted and planned by the city rather than by the owner, in order to insure the harmonious growth of the community.

The convenience and attractiveness of the German city is due to the fact that the city treats the land on which it is built as a whole. It lays out suburbs for a generation in advance of building. It determines the width, style, character of streets. The city controls the land, the buildings, the street and public places for all people and for all time. The city restrains the lawlessness of property just as it restrains the lawlessness of the individual.

The city of Washington is an example of a city that controlled its physical environment in advance of building. It was laid out more than a hundred years ago for a community of 800,000 people. Sites for public buildings were provided. Streets, parks, gardens, and open spaces were selected far in advance of any building. The water front was reserved for the community as it should have been in all cities. The width, style, and character of streets, as well as building restrictions were fixed in the engineer's plan. Recently the railways, the terminals, and stations were made an integral part of the plan. In consequence Washington grew harmoniously. It escaped the costly blunders which confront other cities. For all time Washington is saved from the monotony, the congestion, and the street disorder of the average American city. It is probably the best example of formal planning in the world. What L'Enfant did for the capital of the nation might have been done for every one of our cities had we but had the prescience to do so.

Streets, too, are part of the physical foundations of a city. They are the circulatory system of the community. They are a matter of less concern in America than are our sewers. Yet they add to or subtract from our comfort and convenience, more than anything else save the houses we live in. Streets can be given endless charm, beauty, dignity. They can be built as the Greeks built streets, as Louis XIV and the two Napoleons built the streets of Paris, as streets are being built in Germany today, as things of profound concern to a city.

In the years which followed the Franco-Prussian War the German city was threatened by the rapid growth of the factory system, with the license of land speculators, builders, and factory owners, just as were our own. But Germany courageously faced these problems, just as she faced her condition after the defeat of Prussia by Napoleon. She protested against the spoliation of her cities by the individual and set about to prevent it. City planning grew out of this protest. The cities rejected the American gridiron type of streets, adapted by land speculators interested only in the largest possible profits. For the speculators' streets the city substituted highways, planned with an eye to easy circulation, to convenience, to beauty, to charm. The streets of the modern German city are works of art. The city also controlled the factory, locating where it willed, irrespective of the comfort of the community; it controlled the tenement owner and the slum with the disease, vice, and crime which they produce. Germany turned her trained intelligence to the control of the physical side of the city; to the control of property, as we control persons whose license is inimical to the community. Private property was subordinated to humanity, while the speculator, builder, and factory owner were required to use their own as the community decreed.

When we think of city planning in this country we think of city centers like those of Cleveland, Denver, Rochester, and other cities; we think of the city beautiful, possibly of a well-planned suburb. Or we have in mind a street-widening project or possibly some big commercial planning undertaking like that of Chicago. First in Germany and now in France and England city planning has become a far bigger idea than this; it is more comprehensive than all these combined. A much better phrase to describe city planning is city building; the build-

ing of a city for all the people, for all business, for the future as well as today.

The big difference between the German city and our own is not a difference in honesty. Nor is it a difference of efficiency. The thing that sets off the German city as the most finished in the world is the fact that it is built as we build World's Fairs for fugitive pleasure; as architects design office buildings, or as a private individual lays off a private estate. The city is built as a whole with a conscious realization of its unity, of its possibilities of good as well as its possibilities of evil.

* * *

THE HOPE OF DEMOCRACY

THE twentieth century opens with two distinguishing features — the dominant city and militant democracy. These phenomena are not confined to America. They characterize England, Germany, France, Belgium, and Italy. These features are permanent. This is assured by the nature of things. The life, the industry, the culture of the future will be urbanized, even though some revolution in the means of transit should lead to a decentralization of population. The city may change in many ways — undoubtedly it will. In the city of ten or possibly twenty million people there will be a redistribution of centers, possibly a redivision of political functions. But, in a historical sense, the city has resumed the commanding position which it enjoyed in the days of Athens, Rome, and the mediaeval towns.

In external form and appearance, and methods of administration, the modern city does not differ greatly from its early

prototype. The features common to both are a close association of mankind with many cooperative activities. Nor does the analogy stop here, for in every age the great cities of the world have enjoyed a certain degree of freedom; of local control over the conduct of their affairs. In Athens, Rome, and the Italian cities there were democratic forms and a popular flavor to the government, while the free cities of the Middle Ages were private corporations of the merchants, handworkers, and tradesmen, whose guild organizations elected the magistrates, the mayor, and the aldermen, and through this representation of special interests limited the power of the nobles and the feudal system.

The great difference between the twentieth-century city and those of the past lies in our legalized freedom; in universal education; in an organized machinery backed by years of tradition; but especially in the social instincts and in-

Reprinted with the permission of Charles Scribner's Sons from *The City: The Hope of Democracy* (New York, 1909), pp. 300–313, by Frederic C. Howe.

dustrial background of the present. Democracy, rather than class or business interest, is becoming intelligently organized. In this respect the twentieth century marks the dawning of an epoch in Western civilization. Our politics are reflecting this change. Never before has society been able to better its own condition so easily through the agency of government. The ready responsiveness of democracy, under the close association which the city involves, forecasts a movement for the improvement of human society more hopeful than anything the world has known.

In the past, too, the political unit has been the state, and the theories of philosophers, of the socialist, and the individualist have had in mind a centralized organization, working downwards from the top to the individual.

But a shifting of emphasis has taken place. The tendencies of the present day are towards decentralization, in which the city will command an increasing share of attention. This is apparent in England, where the new democracy at work within the city is rapidly socializing industry with the conscious aim of improving the conditions of life. The same is true of all these reform movements in America that have involved the cooperation of the people.

Everywhere matters affecting the individual in his domestic relations are commanding increased attention. Present-day politics are concerning themselves with the elevation of the standard of living, with equality of opportunity, with the uplifting of life, and the betterment of those conditions which most intimately affect mankind. And these are almost all municipal matters. They bear only a distant relationship to the state at large. They are domestic in character and are being solved by an appeal to manhood

suffrage and democratic organization. History offers no parallel to this phenomenon. For the cities of the past have been aristocratic centers, capital cities, industrial guilds, or feudal strongholds. Nowhere and at no time has society been organized through manhood suffrage and the ballot, and free to carry out its philosophy or desires by a direct appeal to its members. This is a new force in the world — a force of unmeasured possibilities. And when the scope of the city is borne in mind, the possibilities of this new power of conscious, organized democracy are apparent. Saving as to matters of taxation, of international dealings, of transportation from place to place, of the administration of justice, the city is complete within itself. All other affairs of life, even industry itself, fall within the city's control. And with the unit reduced to the city, and with its functions determined by popular control, as is done in the New England town meeting, the dangers from bureaucratic or distant control are reduced to a minimum. For the city will then expand its activities only in response to the developing demands of the community; it will assume new burdens only as it justifies its abilities to perform them. Every city will be an experiment station, offering new experiences to the world. Just as one by one the services now performed by society have passed from private hands under the control of the city, and have brought increased liberty through the change, so the activities of the future will come in through a demand for a higher standard of life, and a larger equality of opportunity.

This very process is going on in every city. The steps that are being taken are so reasonable that they commend themselves to all. The English official resents the suggestion that his city is socialistic, even though it involves the management of many of those activities which, in America, are now left to private enterprise. The American feels no fear of socialism when his city assumes the disposal of garbage, the supply of water or electricity, the opening up of schools, kindergartens, lodging houses, parks, playgrounds, and bath houses. Yet his father would have rubbed his eyes in amazement at the suggestion of such undertakings being proper fields of public activity. Even the city of Cincinnati, which has built a railroad, is far from a socialistic commonwealth. And yet, no city in the Old or New World, with the possible exception of Manchester, which has aided in the construction of a ship canal, has gone to this extent in its functions. Yet Cincinnati has made a success of this venture. Threatened, as the city believed, by railway discrimination, it secured powers from the state to construct a railroad to the south. The enterprise was carried to a successful completion, and for years has proven not only self-sustaining, but a source of revenue to the city.

All this but indicates the amplitude of powers resident in the city by which it may solve, not only the needs that now confront it, but work out the larger social problems of industry as well. What the final municipal program of the new city will be, one can only conjecture, but that it will be a program making for a better civilization, a larger life, and increased comfort and opportunity, the gradual progression of society gives assurance. That these increased activities will come by gradual steps, approved in time by all, is evidenced by the sanction of experience, which accepts with approval the functions which have thus far been assumed.

It may be said that such a program is inconsistent with what we see about us, with the incompetence, if not the dishonesty, of our public life. But we do not see all the evidence. The average efficiency of public work is probably as high as the average efficiency of private work. Trade statistics show that a large per cent of industrial ventures fail each year. Private as well as public work is performed by human agencies, and is subject to human limitations. And the character of municipal politics is rapidly improving.

How great the advance of recent years has been is proven by a contemplation of the conditions of a generation ago. Then, primaries were ruled by fraud, quite as often by force; then the "plug-ugly" of the ward held the caucus in the rear of a saloon and brutally ejected opposition. Those were the insolent Tweed days.

But we need not go back so far. Within the past decade the gain has been remarkable. Reform has become popular. In city after city it is successful. The people are learning to make use of their political tools. The boss and the machine no longer offend the public in the grosser ways so common a few years since. The press is aiding in this movement. National and local organizations are cooperating to elevate public opinion. Better men are entering politics, while the people are learning that the ballot offers a means of redress for the worst abuses. Some of the most hopeless cities have been roused to effective action, and reform has won surprising victories in New York, Pittsburg, Baltimore, Chicago, Cleveland, Detroit, and elsewhere.

When we contemplate these things as well as the former feeling of impotence on the part of the citizen, the recent purification of the ballot, and the substantial gain which has been made in our cities, are little short of revolutionary. Corruption still exists, it is true, as do fraud, bribery, and the more subtle forms of control. But even these are being driven out into the light.

In late years all this has been converted into more respectable forms, and in the process has become even more dangerous to the state. For it is buttressed by those in high places and ramifies into classes who decry the corruption of our life without appreciating their own participation in it. When one contemplates the similarity of conditions in city after city, there seems to be an intelligent adaptation of method by some central power. But this is not true. The similarity which prevails is not the result of concerted action, it is the logical adjustment of political agencies to the use of the private interests, grouped about the great franchise corporations of the nation. And this merging of business and politics, this weaving of private interests into the warp of party organization, has created a system of government; a system that has further entrenched itself through the centralizing tendencies observable in government during the past twenty years. This tendency to centralization has been strengthened by our desire to shirk the burdens of local government and to pass them on from the city to the state, and from the state to the nation at large. The result has been that with every departure from local home rule the opportunity for corruption increases. It opens the chance of control to irresponsible persons. Strict accountability to the people is impossible at a distance. Government that is responsible to local public sentiment cannot fortify itself against that sentiment when aroused, as can a distant executive or a legislature. They cannot be brought to book as can a city council or the mayor.

These tendencies to centralization would be checked by a return to local self-government, to municipal home rule, in which the city would be responsible to itself alone. Then the city would hold its own destiny in its hands, and unless we are ready to believe that the forces of evil are more potent than those of good, that those who desire corrupt government are more numerous than those who desire reform, the outcome of this replacement of responsibility on the shoulders of the people cannot be questioned.

Still other considerations than these of the welfare of the city demand local home rule. The urban population of the United States now comprises one-third of the whole. In the Eastern States it exceeds one-half, and is frequently as much as two-thirds, of the population. If our cities are corrupt, the larger divisions will reflect this corruption. Conversely, anything which will purify the source of the evil will destroy the evil as well. And through the divorce of the city from the state, the power of the senatorial and the state machine will be broken. By this means the city will be free to isolate its politics. Then public sentiment will be elevated and the chain of interests which ramify from the capital at Washington back to city, town, and hamlet will be broken; then a new constituency will come into existence, which, in turn, will elevate the tone of state and national affairs as well.

Just as this political hegemony can be shattered by the release of the city from state control, so municipal politics will be purified by the elimination of the cause of its corruption. The city is not menaced by the people. Popular government has justified many of its promises in so far as it has remained popular. Democracy has been drugged by privileged wealth, and the means of relief are through the resumption of those privileges by the people.

Within the past few years the steam-railway systems of America have been consolidated into a half-dozen master hands. During the same period the street railways and gas companies have been syndicated by a group of New York and Philadelphia capitalists. The same is true of the telephone, as well as of electric light and power. These interests are united by business, social, and political ties that enable them to work as one man in the organization of national, state, and city affairs. Through this unity of power the great natural monopolies of America have become identified with a few men, and these men, through the ramifications of their interests, have been able to develop a system of government which is buttressed on the one hand by the United States Senate and on the other hand by the control of the party in state, county, and city. It is these interests that are responsible for most of the corruption of our cities. For in city after city the conditions are the same. And even were the positive proof lacking, the necessity of it all supplies the explanation. For the franchise corporation is a natural monopoly, exclusive in its service. The value of its securities lies in a grant from the city, rather than in the investment made. The volume of securities which may be issued depends upon the maintenance of this monopoly — the prevention of regulation or competition, and the keeping down of taxes.

There can be no other cause which explains the corruption. The corporation enjoys perpetual succession. Its life exceeds in duration that of the individual. It alone, yesterday, today, tomorrow, is interested in maintaining the *status quo*. Other corrupting influences are transient and occasional. And none save the privileged interests can afford the outlay necessary to secure political control. For the gains enjoyed are measured in millions.

When, in the criminal law, the evidence accumulates to a certainty; when in addition to the evidence the motive appears and cannot be questioned; when the means to be employed are at hand and the goods are found in the possession of the accused; when all these things conjoin; when, in addition, one influence after another can be excluded as inadequate, then the conviction passes beyond a reasonable doubt.

Such is the nature of the proof that it is franchises, grants, and privileges that have subverted our cities and substituted for democracy a system of business government. It is this that has alienated much of the talent and intelligence of the community and made reform a class struggle, and democracy a thing many despair of.

Many there are who question the ability of democracy to solve the problems of city life along the lines indicated. To some this is not so much reasoned conviction as indolent disinclination to assume the burdens involved. It is so much easier to rely on the boss, the party, and the system which has been inaugurated. Yet, the testimony of all experience shows that society has constantly moved onward through forces from below. The great advances in government have been achieved through the common people slowly breaking down privilege after privilege in the onward movement of human liberty. The lesson of our present industrial achievement is the same. The captain of industry has come up from the sod and the mill. He has exemplified the law of nature, which is as active in government as it is in his own career.

The great problem now before the

American people is, how can opportunity be kept open; how can industry be saved from privilege; how can our politics be left to the unimpeded action of talent and ability? This is the problem which the city has to solve, even more than the state or the nation. For in the city the life of the future is to be found. Already the burden of mere existence taxes to the uttermost the energy of an increasing mass of the population. This burden arises in large measure through the increased cost of living, which, in turn, is traceable to rent, to transit, to light, heat, and water, the great natural monopolies, whose values the city creates.

With these services, along with the ground rents of our cities, socialized, the standard of living would be elevated, while through cooperative agencies the city would become in effect an enlarged home, offering to its members many of the comforts and conveniences that are now denied to any save a few. With these opportunities enlarged, the love and affection of the citizen for the city would increase, which, in turn, would bring about a purification of our politics that cannot be obtained so long as the influence of the rich and privileged classes is united against the community.

With such a program achieved, democracy would cease to be a class struggle. There would be created a union of all the people, seeking in conscious ways the betterment of human conditions. Then the merit system, the party, the ballot, the charter, would be reformed by common demand; for then there would be no class, no powerful influence, whose control of the government was dependent upon the persistence of the *status quo*. With home rule secured, with popular control attained, with the city free to determine what activities it will undertake, and what shall be its sources of revenue, then the city will be consciously allied to definite ideals, and the new civilization, which is the hope as well as the problem of democracy, will be open to realization.

IV. URBANIZATION AND THE SHAPING OF TWENTIETH-CENTURY AMERICA

Harvey Wish: URBANISM AND THE CHURCH

Harvey Wish, a highly regarded social and intellectual historian at Western Reserve University, discusses the great impact of the industrial city on the church in America. Covering the major church leaders between 1865 and 1917, he investigates such trends as increased interdenominationalism, agnosticism, the founding of the Christian Science Church, and the growth of the "institutional church."

THE growth of the metropolis, with all that it implied in secularism and anti-traditionalism, gave the churches the greatest challenge in their history. Yet the foreign visitor was impressed by all the external signs of the majestic victory of religion in America between Appomattox and Sarajevo. Never had the urban churches, enriched by the captains of industry, been so crowded; if the modern Gothic buildings with their expensive organs did not outshine the art of the medieval cathedrals, it was not for lack of money; and never before had theological schools, Sunday schools, missions, and church charities attained such dimensions and prosperity in this country. Church attendance figures soared in geometrical ratio, despite the secular world of Charles Darwin, Robert Ingersoll, and Jacques Loeb.

The shift of immigration sources in this era from Northwestern Europe, where Protestants predominated, to Southeastern Europe, with its huge Catholic and Jewish elements, gave the metropolis a large non-Protestant quality.

Catholics and Protestants, Jews and Gentiles, believers and atheists rubbed shoulders in an intimacy foreign to rural society. If the Utopian religious cultists of the mid-century had been unable to shield their followers from error through isolated settlements, how could each urban church retain its unique doctrinal differences when denominational intermarriages daily reflected biological rather than religious promptings? *Interdenominationalism* of the Y.M.C.A. type was inevitable under these circumstances.

In the rootless industrial city, workingmen built their dingy homes around their workplaces and factories. They had little leisure left for church affairs. Low wages, sickness, and joblessness were apt to be more real than the fires of hell and the bliss of eternal salvation. Drink, gambling, and prostitution flourished in this environment. To the perplexed, socialism seemed a more convincing panacea than did personal regeneration. To aid in this difficult task of garnering souls, both Protestant and Catholic churches invoked the social gospel, which meant that the social order was to be transformed into a kingdom of righteousness on earth based upon the social teachings of Jesus. To vie with the attractions of gregarious

From *Society and Thought in Modern America* (New York, 1952), pp. 148–173, by Harvey Wish. Copyright 1952. Used by permission of David McKay Company, Inc.

city life as well as to solve the social evils, there arose, especially after 1890, the "institutional church," handsomely outfitted with welfare services, game and club rooms, and classes for the foreign-born.

The urban intellectuals, even more than the workmen, led the trek away from the church. This generation debated over and over again the problem of reconciling modern science with religion and failed to resolve its secret doubts, even while reaffirming the unity of both. Before the Civil War certain German theological schools fostered "scientific criticism" of the Bible. David Friedrich Strauss of Tübingen shocked the orthodox world in 1835 with his naturalistic "higher criticism" of the Bible and of Christ, in his *Life of Jesus*. Revelation, miracles, and the supernatural suffered their most severe attacks since the time of Voltaire. Protestantism, leaning heavily on the doctrine that the Bible was literally inspired and the sole authority for religion, staggered under the attacks of the "higher critics" upon the origin and development of Christian sacred writings. Scholars, armed with vast linguistic knowledge, challenged the accuracy and authorship of various biblical texts, and anthropologists like Edward Tylor and James Frazer in Britain undermined the assumptions of orthodoxy through the new science of "comparative religion." Frazer's monumental work, *The Golden Bough* (1890), a critical collection of religious and superstitious practices and beliefs, stimulated the reader's impression that Christianity consisted of myths analogous to those of primitive religions.

To the Bible literalists, science was definitely at war with religion. Sir Charles Lyell, the geologist, had already disturbed the Bible literalists by showing that the earth was far older than the mere six thousand years or so suggested by clerical calculations of the date of creation. He had pointed out that any analysis of geological processes proved that the earth had a far greater antiquity than the year 4004 B.C. But the greatest blow to the literalists came from Darwin's *Origin of Species* (1859) and *Descent of Man* (1871). Darwin's theory of natural selection gave the *coup de grâce* in many minds to the idea that man was literally created in the physical image of God. Evolution implied that man was an imperfect product that had developed from some humble amoeba. There seemed cold comfort in the impersonal God whom the deterministic scientists had resurrected from the eighteenth century Deists. This concept of God might please secularists, but it offered no attraction whatever to those who believed in the efficacy of prayer and miracles to correct the inequities of life.

Darwin needed all the help of American philosophers like John Fiske and scientists like Asa Gray to reconcile the idea of divine purpose in the universe with the blind determinism implied in his idea that chance biological variations are selected for survival by the impersonal agency of the environment. Even Darwin, who was too optimistic to believe that "this magnificent world," as he put it, could be the product of blind chance, doubted that God was interested in deciding upon what species were to survive. Many of the organic variations were too useless, he felt, to be the result of special design and merely reflected a struggle for existence. To him the philosophic problem of chance versus design was insoluble. Such reasoning may have led William James and the pragmatists to decide that the search for absolute certainties was futile and that it was enough to know how ideas "worked" in concrete situations.

The impact of evolutionary thought on religion led theologians to make several kinds of intellectual adjustment. Among liberal Protestants, Darwinism and the "higher criticism" were the parents of Modernism which looked upon religious truths as evolutionary, adapting themselves to changing conditions, rather than acting as eternally fixed dogmas. Modernism stimulated the growth of liberal Christianity beyond the confines of Unitarianism and Emersonian transcendentalism. Progressive Protestant theologians, interested in solving the urban problems of labor and poverty, were attracted to a "social gospel" based on evolutionary ideas, particularly as implied in the doctrine of the immanence of God in human society. According to the leading exponents of the social gospel, the evolutionists had proved that God was part of a changing cosmic process and that His divine plan was unfolded in the progress of man upward to an ever higher stage. From this idea, it was easy to reach the conclusion that God's design involved the early emergence of a kingdom of righteousness on earth no less than in heaven. Unlike the millennialist, who simply waited for the Second Coming, the social gospeler believed that the kingdom would come through the intelligent planning of religious men.

Catholicism escaped much of the revolutionary impact of secularism, for it had never shared the biblical literalism of orthodox Protestantism, but rested instead upon the teachings of church tradition, spiritual revelations, and miracles. Heresies like Modernism, schisms, and intellectual deviations could be felled at a blow by the spiritual weapons of the Vatican, ranging from doctrinal encyclicals to excommunications. Catholics contended that science, rightly construed, could not possibly challenge religious dogmas. The *Catholic Encyclopedia* held that the human soul, being of a spiritual nature, could not have evolved from that of the brute; and that a distinction must be made between "the theory of evolution as based on theistic principles and as based on a materialistic and atheistic foundation." To the author of the *Encyclopedia* article Darwin's theory of natural selection was open to scientific criticism as well.

Among the liberal Protestants who clung to economic conservatism rather than the social gospel were a number of fashionable preachers of the Gilded Age who minimized the labor problem but exalted the new science. The best-known of these is Henry Ward Beecher, minister of the well-to-do Plymouth Church in Brooklyn. This remarkable brother of the immortal Harriet had steadily lost whatever he may have once had of the prewar tradition of social dissent. During the Panic of 1873, he refused to admit that there was any basic social maladjustment in the existence of millions of unemployed and the breadlines that taxed the resources of urban churches everywhere. However, he was outspoken in his denunciation of unions, strikes, and labor violence. A *New York Times* reporter in 1877 noted these defiant words of the Great Preacher:

The trade union, originated under the European system, destroys liberty . . . I do not say that a dollar a day is enough to support . . . a man and five children if a man would insist on smoking and drinking beer. . . . But the man who cannot live on bread and water is not fit to live.

His biographer, Paxton Hibben, relates that thirty police and a corps of secret service men guarded Beecher during this harangue. While Plymouth Church applauded, critical journalists caricatured him and his $20,000-a-year salary.

This son of strict old Lyman Beecher moved ever farther from the historic Calvinism and ideals of his Congregationalist background. While he clung to the language of the supernatural, his theology became increasingly "liberal" and "humanistic" in the crudest sense, betraying the most flagrant philosophical inconsistencies. His optimistic sermons made "love" their cardinal point, but he did not extend its application to the laboring man. He reassured his wealthy congregation that the Bible must not be taken too literally in its strictures upon the rich man's entering heaven. He could eulogize the militant agnostic, Colonel Robert Ingersoll (whose economic views coincided with his own) and, at the same time, tell his listeners that he could not accept predestination or Hell. Following closely in the footsteps of several prominent Anglican churchmen who, in 1877, had repudiated the traditional concept of Hell, Beecher was able to create a new sensation in the American pulpit — there were many of these "shockers" in his technique — by saying that he could not believe that God could be so malign as to destroy men in the fires of Hell like insects over a fire. In 1882, he publicly explained his convenient pragmatic theology to the Congregational Association:

I gradually formed a theology by practice — by trying it on, and the things that really did God's work in the hearts of men I set down as good theology, and the things that did not, *whether they were true or not, they were not true to me.*

He converted innumerable followers to an early acceptance of evolution and to his Spencerian version of "liberal religion." Religion to him was an adventure in personal well-being — limited to the middle class in its material benefits — and it was simple for Beecher to raise evolution to the status of a spiritual revelation, "God's thought in the evolution of matter." These ideas appeared in his exuberant book, *Evolution and Religion* (1885). He took issue with the "bigoted theologists, ignorant pietists, jealous churchmen," and unintelligent men who ridiculed Lyell's geology and Darwin's biology.

In an age of middle-class complacency, Beecher made a dogma of self-congratulation; at a time when severe social dislocations had been let loose by industrialism and crowded cities, he diverted the Christian doctrine of social responsibility into the irresponsibility of Spencerian laissez faire and the uncritical acceptance of the inevitability of social progress. Science was in effect equated with God and became a popular religion despite its lack of ethical content.

2

Rural Protestants and their orthodox allies in the cities rebelled against the "modernist" liberals and their faith in science as a guide to spiritual values. In many congregations liberals and conservatives quarreled, being too often held together only by their mutual stake in church property. By the twentieth century the conservatives had organized themselves into "fundamentalist" sects wherever it was necessary. In 1910, these religious authoritarians issued a booklet assailing Modernism, *The Fundamentals; a Testimony to the Truth,* which contained an uncompromising statement of fundamentalist views as against heresy. This pamphlet stressed five points of doctrine: the virgin birth of Christ, the resurrection, the imminent Second Coming, the atonement for man's sins by Christ's sacrifice, and the inerrancy of the Bible. As for the Catholic Church, its rejection of Modernism was thorough; papal encyclicals emphatically denounced this as a flagrant heresy to be avoided by the faithful.

Not a few urban intellectuals and working-class radicals espoused a far more anti-traditional viewpoint than Modernism. This was the agnosticism of Robert Ingersoll and his followers. In England, Thomas Henry Huxley, an English biologist whose militant championship of evolution on the public platform won him the title, "Darwin's bulldog," attacked dogmatic theology in the name of "agnosticism." He defined this as a scientific attitude of suspended judgment in which the individual finds a lack of evidence to affirm the existence of God or a life after death. In effect this meant a denial of the historic mission of the Church and a reversion to Voltaire in its militant anti-clericalism.

The amazing popularity of Robert Green Ingersoll (1833–99), dubbed "the great agnostic," suggests the increased tolerance of his generation to an irreligious position hitherto unforgivable in a major public figure. In antebellum times, it is true, radical reformers like Robert Dale Owen and Frances Wright had organized the "Free Enquirers" to oppose organized religion as well as to promote sweeping plans of social reconstruction. A sprinkling of "free-thinkers" had always infiltrated American radical thought in previous generations.

However, Ingersoll, like Voltaire, had no intention of assaulting the bastions of economic orthodoxy, for he was the friend and legal counsel of the mighty in business industry. He had broken with the Congregationalism of his minister-father in which he had been reared.

Gifted with a flair for spread-eagle oratory, and buttressed by an impressive Civil War record, he became a politician and a wealthy lawyer with a long list of legal victories won before impressionable jurors. Not the least of his laurels was his masterly and successful defense of the defendants in the "Star Route" scandals involving large-scale fraud against the government in the compensation of mail contractors. So orthodox were the views of Ingersoll in politics and economics that he might possibly have reached the highest office had his irreligious views not been a barrier to his "availability." He could bury vital economic issues beneath the most contagious emotional appeals of the "bloody shirt" variety, keeping green the memories of Civil War sectional hates. Best remembered as a service to his party was his nomination of James G. Blaine in 1876 as the Republican presidential candidate. His flattering characterization of the shifty Blaine as the Plumed Knight caught the imagination of his generation.

Influenced by Darwin, Huxley, and the "higher criticism" movement against the Bible's infallibility, he expounded his agnosticism before huge crowds for thirty years, attracting the young lawyer, Clarence Darrow, among many other liberals, to his position. His forceful oratory as well as his heterodox ideas drew audiences for such lecture topics as "Some Mistakes of Moses" and "Why I Am an Agnostic." In the latter speech he defined the agnostic, "He gives up the hope of ascertaining first or final causes, of comprehending the supernatural, or of conceiving of an infinite personality." To him the world was without beginning and would be without end; religion and morals were in large part the product of soil, climate, and circumstance. He declared that Shakespeare was preferable to the prophets from a literary point of view and that Darwin and Humboldt were superior to the author of Genesis as scientists. Constantly he attacked organized religion. "With sword and flame, it destroyed the brave and thoughtful men who told the truth. It was the enemy of investigation and reason. Faith and fiction were in partnership." Unlike the agnostics and atheists among the working-class socialists, he avoided any criticism of the churches for conservative economic tenets.

3

The cityward movement challenged the evangelical exhorters who discarded formal theology for a simple emotional appeal to the uprooted semi-literate masses. Foremost among those to retain the soul-saving tradition of the camp meeting, though in a more dignified form, was Dwight L. Moody, once a Boston shoe salesman, but active in city missionary work and Sunday school teaching since the 1850's. He served as secretary of the Chicago Y.M.C.A. and during the Civil War became an active missionary on the field for the United States Christian Commission. Never ordained as a minister and lacking all but rudimentary book learning, he proved nevertheless one of the most effective preachers of all time. To the agnostics and Modernists who found inconsistencies in the Bible, he replied emphatically, "The Bible was not made to understand!"

In 1870, he met Ira David Sankey, a minor revenue clerk who desired above everything to use his powerful dramatic voice in winning souls. Moody and Sankey toured the British Isles as well as the United States and aroused the revivalist spirit wherever they went. The *New York Times* declared in 1876, "A new hope has lifted up hundreds of human beings; a new consolation has come to the sorrowful; and a better principle has entered the sordid life of the day through the labors of these plain men." Moody seemed to be a new John Wesley, eager to inspire religious excitement without the extremes of hysteria or the "jerks." Women often credited their conversions to the effect of a hymn sung by Sankey such as "Hold the Fort," "Watching and Waiting," and "Ninety and Nine." Moody recalled he had heard "Rock of Ages" once a day for six years.

These evangelists avoided the pressing economic questions of the day. Wall Street, like the East Side slums, had souls to save and the advantages of the world to come appeared far too great for quarrels over temporary advantages in this one. The wealthy as well as the poor contributed heavily to Moody's insistent fund-raising campaigns in behalf of his large chain of educational institutions. In 1889, he had built a citadel of evangelical training in the (Moody) Bible Institute for Home and Foreign Missions in Chicago. At his birthplace and residence, Northfield, Massachusetts, he introduced annual conferences of church workers and students. A master of publicity — his critics called him the Barnum of religion — he scattered tons of religious tracts wherever he went. When he died in 1899 the statistically-minded estimated that he had carried his gospel messages fully a million miles, addressed 100,000,-000 people, and prayed directly with 750,000 sinners. Admirers insisted that he had reduced the population of hell by a million souls.

Moody's earnest words, spoken in rapid conversational style while he used only the simplest of gestures, deeply affected his listeners and drew masses back to the "Old Time Religion." Sankey sat at the organ, always facing the congregation and eagerly watching their expressions. He played the beloved gospel hymns and sang impressively like a basso profundo of the opera.

In the early twentieth century, evangelism had its most sensational champion in Billy Sunday, a professional baseball player from Iowa. Although like Moody, he came to evangelical work through the Y.M.C.A., there was almost none of Moody's dignity in his pulpit manner, despite the fact that he was actually ordained a Presbyterian minister in 1903. In his Philadelphia pulpit Billy Sunday wound up like a baseball pitcher and exhorted the audience "to put it over the plate for Jesus." But he, too, like Moody, ignored the basic economic and social abuses of his day except for his heated campaign against the saloon. To the fundamentalist, Sabbath-breaking and drink were the chief social problems of the times.

4

The Young Men's Christian Association, which had provided such militants as Moody, Sunday, and Anthony Comstock, had been founded in England in 1844 by George Williams and had been sponsored by men of at least four different Protestant denominations. It was an interdenominational laymen's movement to convert youth, particularly those spiritually adrift in the cities, to religion. The movement took root in America in 1851 with the founding of the Boston chapter and grew into vast national and international dimensions. The Y.M.C.A. did much to promote the religious revival of 1857–58, which penetrated into the financial districts as well as the homes of the humble, and it organized charities for the poor and nursing aid for the sick.

Beginning in 1868, "active" members were expected to be members in good standing of evangelical churches, while others might join as "associate" members, providing they were of good moral character. Each branch centered around the personality of a vigorous secretary. The New York "Y" introduced physical education, thereby giving an important impetus to the adoption of German calisthenics in the public schools of the nation. To rally the youth for religion and to reconcile class and race, the "Y" steadily expanded its Sunday school program to absorb a variety of social activities, such as reading rooms, clubs and classes of all types, as well as gymnastics. During the Civil War the various Y.M.C.A. groups united to form the United States Christian Commission to furnish to the soldiers wholesome books and tracts, both religious and secular. Such services were expanded to include recreation in the Spanish-American War and World War I.

Another such English institution transplanted to New York in 1858 was the Young Women's Christian Association. This, too, had urban as well as religious roots. Originally, women were attracted to the idea of a large prayer group for their sex. Too often they had been frowned upon or discriminated against in the conduct of missionary and evangelical work. The founders, such as Emma Robarts in England, cited their aim in the biblical thought that "thy sons and thy daughters shall prophesy." Their purpose was "to labor for the temporal, moral, and religious welfare of young self-supporting women." In 1887, after William T. Stead had publicized the immorality prevalent among girls who earned a pittance in industry, the London Y.W.C.A. added a strong social program to this limited gospel movement. Out of this grew women's hostels, the Traveller's Aid Society, and the Park Mission.

After 1866, the American Y.W.C.A.,

like others elsewhere, modeled their organizational structure after the Y.M.C.A. Physical education, schooling in many liberal and applied subjects, and social and recreational activities were added to religious training. The American Y.W.C.A. pioneered with the cafeteria idea in its Kansas City branch. Its main purpose was to reduce food prices for working girls by eliminating as much of the service cost as possible. From Kansas City the cafeteria system moved eastward and became popular both in "Y" circles and outside by 1900. So successful was the Y.W.C.A. in this country that it was able to report in 1910 a total membership of close to a quarter of a million spread over 196 city associations. Many hundreds were enrolled in mission study classes. Troubled immigrant women frequently turned to the "Y" for advice and assistance.

Since the battle for church survival in a secular age depended upon the success of youth programs, Protestants experimented with other institutions besides the two "Y" movements. The leading Methodist denominations forged their instrument in the Epworth League, originating in 1872 in Philadelphia from a group organized by the Reverend T. B. Neely of the Fifty-first Street Methodist Episcopal Church. The most remarkably successful of the religious youth groups was the Young People's Society of Christian Endeavor. In February, 1881, the Reverend Francis E. Clark founded the first chapter at his Williston Congregational Church in Portland, Maine. By 1911, the Society had become an interdenominational movement of nearly 2,-700,000 American members while over 1,200,000 more belonged to Canadian and overseas chapters — a grand total of nearly four million young men and women. The Christian Endeavor pledge

required each member to promise to apply religion through some concrete service, however small, to society. Their motto was "For Christ and the Church" and their activities embraced missions, charities, and social programs. Among the Christian Endeavor principles was this social-economic platform:

Christian endeavor stands for Peace and Good Will among men, and is opposed to all unjust war and unjust industrial strife, as contrary to the principles of the Prince of Peace. "Arbitration and Conciliation" are two of its watchwords for the twentieth century, and an International Christian Brotherhood and a universal language for intercommunication two of its ideals.

5

In a sense the efforts of Protestants to retain their urban membership may be considered as a militant counter-reformation against secularism and indifference. The leaders of this movement originated in industrial England and were the soldiers of the Salvation Army. This movement, like so many others of this period, was interdenominational and therefore tended to minimize dogmatic differences among Protestants in order to achieve the experience of Christian conversion.

The first general and founder of the Salvation Army was William Booth, who had been reared within the Church of England and had joined a band of Wesleyan Methodists as a youthful evangelist. In 1850 he became a minister and thereafter embarked as an independent evangelist in London, bringing his remarkable wife, Catherine, to his aid. He labored for the souls of slum dwellers, drunkards, and the human debris of London. His audiences filled huge tents, theaters, and open fields. "The Christian Mission is the Salvation Army," he once said and this name became fixed in the reorganization of 1880. General Booth invoked "councils of war," moved his evangelists in "corps," and held meetings in "citadels." In seaports, evangelists called themselves "captains." Eventually, *The War Cry* became the official organ of the movement.

From the beginning the Salvation Army realized that hungry and homeless men must first be fed and sheltered before they were ready for a Christian life. Soup kitchens, shelters, and other social institutions quickly evolved. This strategy of combining social with spiritual services was stressed in Booth's book, *Darkest England and the Way Out*. The new and unusually prominent role of women as evangelists owed much to Catherine Booth, who was aware of the precedents set by the Quakers in this direction. By 1890, there were 5000 women officers in the Salvation Army, many wearing the distinctive bonnet fashioned by Catherine herself.

In 1880, the very year that the name Salvation Army was formally adopted, a branch was established in Pennsylvania under Commissioner George Railton and seven women workers from England. Younger members of the Booth family took charge of the American organization. One of the best known, Evangeline Cory Booth, daughter of the founder, held the leadership for thirty years after 1904 and then became the General of the Army. The Army's militant evangelical methods in the United States and elsewhere have been frankly explained by one of the Booths:

The Salvationist's vision of a rebellious world and of perishing souls seems to justify any and every device, however sharp, striking, or even vulgar for attracting, for compelling, the attention of the hardened and in-different to whom his appeal is made. . . . The testimony meeting is described as a "free and easy" and the response of "Amen" as a "volley." Many Army services are punctuated from first to last with joyous exclamations, clapping of hands, laughter, or tears.

One of the best conversion methods had to do with the "mourners' bench," which is said to have been borrowed by William Booth from President Charles Finney of Oberlin, the noted evangelist. This was a row of seats in front of the speaker's platform at which sinners kneeled in token of repentance. This version of the "anxious seat" added a keen dramatic interest to the services. Street marches by the "Hallelujah lasses," their familiar guitars, tambourines, and brass instruments, and lively or sentimental tunes from the Salvation Army Song Books were part of their appeal to prospective converts. Many of these songs were secular in origin but were sung with specially adapted salvationist words. By 1900, the Salvation Army had grown in this country to 700 corps of 20,000 privates commanded by 3000 officers. At this time, too, they were conducting an average of 11,000 weekly meetings with an attendance of over two million people.

After 1890, William Booth's plan for a large-scale welfare program began to unfold. The American branch of the Army helped the derelicts through numerous soup kitchens, old clothes depots, cheap hotels, and homes for alcoholics. Destitute families were housed in special shelters, permitted to buy necessities at cheap food stores, given employment, or aided generously through a loan service. Mothers were sent to maternity homes and cared for through public nursing agencies; unmarried mothers and prostitutes were aided through rescue homes. A special prison-gate bureau helped newly released prisoners to start fresh lives. The salvage of human derelicts was a mighty industry with the Army.

This vast program might be stigmatized as consisting of "palliatives" instead of social reform, but to the destitute it meant immediate sympathetic aid until such time as the nation and the municipalities were ready to shoulder the burden in a more scientific way. For the churches, it meant vast recruits of members, and for society, it led to the physical as well as spiritual rehabilitation of a submerged class that normally had no outlets but drink and unbridled sensualism.

In 1896, General Ballington Booth and his wife led a group of secessionists out of the Salvation Army to form an exclusively American movement with a more democratic internal structure, the Volunteers of America. They continued the military paraphernalia on a lesser scale, but avoided direct competition with the churches. In their evangelical work they stressed conversion among convicts and alcoholics. Their Volunteer Prison League enrolled thousands of convicts who pledged themselves to a disciplined Christian life. Ex-convicts were assisted to find secure niches in society where the stigma of their past might not force them back into criminal acts.

6

The long dreary depression eras of 1873 and 1893 and the violent nationwide strikes associated with them led many thoughtful clergymen to revise their exclusive emphasis on otherworldliness. Besides, the rapid growth of Marxist socialism among laborers during the 1880's and afterwards alarmed churchmen in both Europe and America. Radical clubs ridiculed the clergyman's promises of salvation as "pie in the sky" and in Marxian terms assailed religion as an opiate for the people to divert attention from the class struggle. After 1890, many Protestants and Catholics devoted serious attention to formulating a "social gospel," which taught that the principles of Christianity were broad enough to support a just social order of a cooperative nature. For them, the traditional kingdom of heaven could not be allowed to obscure the hope of a kingdom of righteousness on earth.

Socially-minded critics attacked the orthodox who were only concerned with the problem of personal redemption without realizing that society, too, must be redeemed from its economic abuses. They were dissatisfied with the limited ascetic program of the churches — temperance, Sabbatarianism, Comstockian morality, and persistent campaigns to halt smoking and card-playing. Within the traditional church doctrine of stewardship, churchmen insisted that all wealth is held and administered for the common good. Catholics recurred to the pre-capitalistic Christian society of the medieval guild community with its subordination to the common good — in theory at least — of profits and competitive conflict. Social gospelers also found theological sanctions in the doctrine that God was immanent in human society — a formula that tended to blur the usually sharp distinctions between secular and religious interests.

England directly influenced the social gospel movement and its institutions, for her urban-industrial problems resembled those of the United States in an accentuated form. Within the Church of England a group of clerics and laymen, led by Frederick D. Maurice, took up where Chartism had left off in 1848 to rebel against laissez-faire capitalism and to demand that the economic order conform to Christian ethics within a cooperative system. Best-known of these "Christian Socialists" to American readers was the clergyman-novelist Charles Kingsley, who wrote *Alton Locke* (1850) and *Yeast* (1851) to picture working-class conditions. In England, too, there was the esthetic and individualistic Socialism of William Morris and John Ruskin. These men seldom went beyond plans or experiments for a producer's or consumer's cooperative, but they influenced the gradualist tradition of the Fabian Socialists and the British Labour Party. From England, too, came the settlement movement, which was originated by an Anglican vicar, Samuel A. Barnett, as an experiment in London slum rehabilitation. Barnett founded Toynbee Hall in 1884 to provide university-trained "residents" in a poor district of the East End. Essentially, all these activities were merely middle-class efforts to direct the economic salvation of the working classes. Some groups of the Christian Socialists were even cool to secular trade-union movements and none favored the revolutionary Marxist or anarchist panaceas for the ills of the world.

Much more influential upon the later Christian Socialist movement was Washington Gladden, outspoken pastor of the First Congregational Church in Columbus, Ohio. He insisted that now that slavery had been abolished, the emancipation of labor came next and the social problem was therefore primary. Active in various municipal and social reforms, he expressed his conviction that the laborer's real wages had declined during 1860-86 and were still falling. He was one of the early clerical figures to give the weight of church support to trade unions and the right to strike; his wrath fell upon the abuses of unregulated economic competition. Adam Smith and classical economics, he charged, had come to replace the Bible. His numerous

books, such as *Applied Christianity* (1886), popularized the social gospel. In 1891 appeared his challenging exposition of religious Modernism in *Who Wrote the Bible?*

While Gladden offered little in the way of concrete reforms, the developing English movement of Christian Socialism crossed the Atlantic and gave a program to many American social gospelers. One of these American leaders of Christian Socialism was an Episcopal clergyman of Boston, William D. P. Bliss, who named his organization the Church of the Carpenter and even joined the Knights of Labor. Like other radical clergymen, he had been attracted at first by Edward Bellamy's Utopian Socialist book *Looking Backward, 2000-1887* (1888), in which the leading character awakens in the midst of a socialist society that plans almost every phase of daily life. However, the secular nature of Bellamy's Nationalist movement led Bliss and other churchmen to turn away and organize in 1889 the Society of Christian Socialists in Boston, editing *The Dawn,* and attacking plutocracy and economic planlessness in favor of a gradualist program of regulation and control of capital.

The greatest name and influence in American Social Christianity was undoubtedly Walter Rauschenbusch, a Baptist clergyman of Rochester, New York, the son of German liberal Forty-eighters. As a young idealistic pastor in New York city's slums, he had seen poverty at first hand; as a result, his religion was imbued with a strong social quality. He had read sympathetically Henry George's single-tax doctrines, Tolstoy's idealistic essays on personal redemption, and John Spargo's socialist writings. He emerged a Christian Socialist, devoted to the goal of a socialist state based on biblical principles.

To Marxians, however, his rejection of

the principles of the class struggle as a cardinal tenet of socialism put him outside the pale of "scientific socialism." Rauschenbusch denounced the jungle philosophy of unregulated competition and proposed a social order in which the profit motive would be replaced by a cooperative ideal. In *Christianizing the Social Order* (1912), written at the height of the Bull Moose movement, he predicted gloomily, "An ever increasing number of people are henceforth to live in a land owned by an ever decreasing number." It was time to turn away from mammonism and corporate control of government and time for all society to experience the exalted sense of personal regeneration that the convert knew.

In his published Yale lectures of 1917, *A Theology for the Social Gospel,* Rauschenbusch formulated the doctrinal basis of Social Christianity. Most popular of all was *The Social Principles of Jesus* (1917). These titles alone suggest the consistent emphasis that he put upon his central tenets of a kingdom of righteousness on earth. Under his leadership Christian Socialists organized the Brotherhood of the Kingdom. More important than this is the fact that, for an entire generation at least, innumerable idealistic young clergymen were profoundly influenced by the social teachings of Rauschenbusch.

No man in the entire Social Christian movement enjoyed so vast an audience as the Reverend Charles Monroe Sheldon of Topeka, Kansas, whose mass appeal as a novelist may justly be compared with that of Harriet Beecher Stowe. A prolific writer of idealistic sketches for denominational papers, this Congregationalist minister knew poverty and unemployment from close observation. In 1896, he published *In His Steps: What Would Jesus Do?* This began with a story related to a congregation by an unem-

ployed youth whose wife had died in a New York tenement. The young man challenged the congregation by asking what Jesus would do if He were a member of this church. After the youth died the aroused pastor asked his congregation to live for a year exactly as they thought Jesus would, regardless of consequences. Thereafter a wholesale transformation took place as members gave up narrow or harmful activities to promote better housing for the poor, mission work, and temperance. So sensational was the success here and abroad of *In His Steps* that the book sold over 100,000 copies in a year and quickly passed the million mark and the story was shown on the motion picture screen in 1936.

The climax of the social gospel movement came in 1908 after Unitarians, Episcopalians, Methodists, Baptists, and Congregationalists had already formed welfare organizations and adopted social principles going beyond the older restricted notions of charity. In May, 1908, the Methodist Episcopal Church issued its famous "Social Creed," which included these principles: industrial conciliation and arbitration; elimination of factory hazards to life and health; the abolition of child labor; protection of women in industry; abolition of the sweat shop; the "gradual and reasonable reduction of the hours of labor to the lowest practical point, with work for all"; and the acquisition of "that degree of leisure for all which is the condition of the highest human life." They advocated a holiday of one day in seven, "a living wage in every industry," and particularly "the highest wage that each industry can afford, and for the most equitable division of the products in industry that can ultimately be devised."

This ambitious program was implemented that same year by the formation of the most important interdenominational group in the history of Protestantism: The Federal Council of the Churches of Christ in America, eventually representing twenty-seven national denominations, including both races, and dealing with practically every problem of human welfare. This organization took over as its own the Social Creed of the Methodists and set up local and state councils to assist it in dealing with national and international questions including evangelical programs, reform of marriage laws, philanthropy, and social legislation. "The Council holds it a Christian duty to make the influence of Christ effective in all human relations," reads a recent semi-official statement; "It draws Christian representatives of management, labor, and agriculture together to consider what light is shed upon their problems by their common Christian commitment." Thus in the twentieth century centrifugal tendencies of Protestantism had been partially checked through such interdenominational forms as the F.C.C.C.A. More and more churches took up the "labor question," investigated strikes sympathetically, or offered their services as labor mediators. The "institutional" church grew after 1890 to include a wide variety of welfare, educational, and recreational activities. Such urban churches often added employment bureaus, charitable relief agencies, kindergartens, gymnasiums, libraries, clubs, dispensaries, soup kitchens, hospitals, and home economics classes. A "Christian sociology" pervaded their philosophy.

7

With the urban emphasis upon interdenominationalism and the social gospel, the birth of new sects became an increasing rarity. One of the most important of the few urban sects that were organized in this period was the Chris-tian Science Church. Appealing to the middle class primarily, it did not take an active role in the social gospel movement. Its emphasis on mental healing, suggesting certain of the therapeutic values of psychoanalysis, seemed well-adapted to uprooted urban culture in which mental adjustments often took physical forms baffling to the techniques of ordinary medicine. This "Church of Christ, Scientist" was chartered in 1879 in Boston by a unique figure in American church history, Mary Baker Eddy, already a woman of fifty-eight.

Mrs. Eddy was born in 1821 on a farm in New Hampshire of a long line of Congregational ancestors. She was largely self-educated, though she had an unmistakably keen native intelligence. Her personal life was not happy, for her first husband died, she divorced her second, and the third, Asa Eddy, whom she loved dearly, died a few years after their marriage. Throughout her early life she had suffered from sudden pains in her spine and chronic invalidism and she had tried the current healing panaceas, including mesmerism and spiritualism. She consulted Phineas P. Quimby of Portland, Maine, regarding her health and thought that she had secured some relief. Quimby used no medicines, but relied upon manipulation and mental suggestion. When he died in 1866, Mrs. Eddy turned to other hopes of cure and became immersed in the idea of the healing mission of Jesus. She had long been interested in the mental factors in illness and hoped to convince the churches to take up her emphasis on faith healing. When this hope failed to materialize, she developed her own church to carry out the principles she had discovered.

In 1875, she published *Science and Health*, which in various revised forms became the textbook of the Christian Science movement. She developed the idea that Jesus came upon earth not only to redeem man from sin, but also from disease. Men must discover "the Christ in us." In one of her most-quoted passages, she said,

There is no life, truth, intelligence, nor substance in matter. All is infinite Mind and its infinite manifestations, for God is All-in-All. Spirit is immortal Truth; matter is mortal error. . . . Spirit is God, and man is His image and likeness. Therefore man is not material; he is spiritual.

This, in a highly condensed form, gave the essence of her teachings. By living the life of a genuine Christian, one might hope to overcome error and unreality, which includes sickness and sin. These cheerful ideas of mind-cure were especially attractive to the optimistic psychology of many Americans. To spread the faith, Mrs. Eddy founded monthly, weekly, and daily newspapers. By 1890, her *Christian Science Journal* advertised the presence of 250 healers, 20 churches, and 90 societies. The phenomenon of a woman at the head of a large church was not new in New England, for Mother Ann Lee had founded Shaker colonies there a century before.

In 1906 a two-million-dollar addition to the Mother Church at Boston was completed. At that time the Boston organization was estimated to have over 40,000 members, and there were at least 25,000 more elsewhere. Two years later the *Christian Science Monitor* appeared; it offered lectures on the faith together with an unusually high level of journalism in which the sections on foreign affairs ranked with the best in the country. It avoided any emphasis on vice or crime and sought to keep a neutral position between capital and labor. In 1910, the eighty-nine-year-old woman who had obviously built up a powerful organization died. Within a few years, her church won many converts in England, Germany, and elsewhere.

8

The American Roman Catholic Church was overwhelmingly recruited from immigrants who found their livelihood in the cities and thus it became predominantly an urban church. Despite the poverty of the newcomers, the hierarchy was able to build parochial schools, churches, colleges, hospitals, and monastic institutions. In addition, the church had to support its own extensive program of charities. Besides the unique Catholic problem of adjusting millions of incoming Irishmen, Bavarians, Italians, Poles, Czechs, Austrians, and others to the American environment, there were also the same problems faced by Protestants: secularism, Marxist socialism, and urban indifference.

In this era the leadership of Cardinal Gibbons was often decisive in Catholic affairs. Without demanding any special status for the large American Catholic population within the Roman Church, he urged the Vatican that the Church must not be stigmatized by Americans as an alien institution. Instead, bishops should be chosen who were in accord with American ideas of democracy. When in 1891 certain nationalistic German Catholics sought a special status for their nationality, the Cardinal successfully fought this "Cahenslyism" as a threat to the homogeneity of American Catholicism. On that occasion a Peter Cahensly had presented a church memorial recommending that each nationality be given its churches, priests, and proportion of bishops according to their respective numbers. Although it had been the prac-

eign language group with a priest who could speak its language, the Cardinal denounced any effort to segregate each group on a rigid nationality basis.

Next to the Cardinal in influence was the very able archbishop of St. Paul, John Ireland. At one time President Roosevelt even intervened indirectly to help the archbishop get a cardinal's hat — an odd activity for a Protestant! Like Cardinal Gibbons, Archbishop Ireland favored an American policy for the church in this country with special emphasis upon an enthusiastic acceptance of political democracy. However, he tended to minimize the great economic problems of the time except to advocate temperance and conservative trade unionism. In 1903, he publicly declared, "I have no fear of great fortunes in the hands of individuals, nor of vast aggregations of capital in the hands of corporations." His friendships with James J. Hill, railroad magnate, and with President McKinley exposed him to the shafts of progressives. Yet he often expressed strong sympathies for organized labor, even remarking on one occasion, "Until their material condition is improved it is futile to speak to them of spiritual life and duties."
tice of the hierarchy to provide each for-

Many Catholic priests and laymen did support radical causes. A particularly significant case was that of Father Edward McGlynn who made ardent speeches in behalf of Henry George and the single tax doctrines. In 1886, the attention of the entire nation was arrested by the news that he had been suspended by his superiors from his priestly duties. When he refused a summons to Rome to defend his opinions, he was excommunicated. However, the decree was revoked by the end of 1892 and he resumed his duties. Father McGlynn's victory encouraged other Catholics to espouse radical labor

reforms. The attitude of the American hierarchy may perhaps be inferred from a significant letter in the Baltimore Cathedral Archives. On July 21, 1894, at the height of the disorders of the Pullman Strike, Archbishop Ireland wrote to Cardinal Gibbons:

The Church must be kept before the American people as the great prop of social order and law — all the more so that Catholics are numerous in strikes and riots. Socialistic ideas have gone into our people and into many of our priests. We have been siding with labor in its grievances: The unthinking ones transgress the golden mean, and rush into war against property.

For Catholics everywhere who hoped for a vigorous program of social action to meet the problems of poverty and materialism, a ready-made creed appeared in the famous papal encyclical, *Rerum Novarum,* issued by Leo XIII in 1891. Pope Leo had been an able social reformer while still a young priest; and some years before issuing the encyclical he had directed that social problems be made a part of the training curriculum for priests. An erudite philosopher with a special interest in the teachings of St. Thomas Aquinas, Pope Leo revived Thomism and thereby gave a new vitality to Catholic philosophy in the ensuing decades. The encyclical condemned laissez faire in industry as unchristian, declared that labor was not a commodity to be bought and sold on the market, upheld the right to organize unions, and asserted the principle of the living wage based upon the needs of the family. Class collaboration, instead of class conflict, was the keynote of the encyclical: "Capital cannot do without labor nor labor without capital." *Rerum Novarum* made slow progress as far as adoption in this country is concerned, but there were many militant Catholic advocates of its ideas.

The American Catholic who devoted his life most effectively and brilliantly to the application of the principles of *Rerum Novarum* was a priestly professor of social economics at Catholic University, Father John A. Ryan. Born of Irish parents in 1869 in a village near St. Paul, he had learned his Populist ideas from rebels like Ignatius Donnelly and from the anti-landlord sentiments of *The Irish World* to which his family had long subscribed. Professor Richard T. Ely of the University of Wisconsin, who may have influenced him, wrote an introduction to Ryan's doctoral dissertation, which appeared in 1906 as *A Living Wage*. This book attracted wide interest and almost certainly left an impression on the thinking of innumerable social reformers.

Father Ryan asserted the principle that no employer had any right to take interest on his investment until all his employees had received a living wage. This he estimated at $600 a year as a minimum subsistence for a family. He later wrote that this book was the first in English to advocate a legally established compulsory minimum wage sufficient for the decent maintenance of the worker's family. Unlike certain other Catholic critics of the economic order, this priest-economist refused to escape to the Middle Ages for a just social order. He believed that Americans had definitely broken with European tradition and would seek their solution in terms of their own experience. "The laborer's right to a living wage," he declared, "is like all other moral rights, based on his intrinsic worth as a person, and on the sacredness of those needs that are essential to the reasonable development of personality." Charity was good, but no substitute for justice. His wage ideas were developed more maturely in *Distributive Justice* (1917), which carried the subtitle, *The Right and Wrong of Our Present Distribution of Wealth.* Throughout his life he combined his scholarly interests with active social work.

The monolithic structure of the Roman Catholic Church made it relatively simple to escape schisms and to deal with heresies and secularist doctrines arising out of the new age of science. In 1864, Pope Pius IX issued the *Syllabus of Errors* to denounce freethinkers, agnostics, materialists, anticlericals, freemasons, and doctrinal liberals. The papal encyclical *Pascendi* (1907) issued by Pope Pius X condemned Modernism as a union of faith with a false philosophy. Inevitably, the cities made some inroads upon orthodoxy, but these were far more than offset by steady accretions of strictly orthodox immigrant groups.

Unlike conservative Protestant churches, the Catholic hierarchy could meet new science unencumbered by any dogmatic belief in the literal truth of the Bible; and while very slow to accept Darwinism they were not compelled to stake the validity of doctrine upon the truth or falsehood of evolution. On the other hand, Protestantism, traditionally consecrated to "justification by faith alone" had moved over — except for a fundamentalist wing — to a humanitarian program ever more devoted to "good works" as a way of salvation. Critics of social Christianity wondered whether churchmen were competent to solve the complex economic problems of contemporary society or were even well-advised to attempt it. Well-to-do congregations resented clerical meddling in the employer's problems; but the fashionable liberal Christianity of Henry Ward Beecher could only end in altogether estranging the working classes from religion.

Christopher Tunnard and Henry Hope Reed:
THE CITY BEAUTIFUL

Beautification of the modern city was one of the greatest challenges which emerged from the Gilded Age. In a chapter from their book, American Skyline, two of our foremost students of city planning, Christopher Tunnard and Henry Hope Reed, discuss how this challenge was met in the years 1880–1910, and describe the legacy which the planners and architects of that era left to the twentieth century.

A FRESH current flowed through the American urban scene in this generation; not all was dedicated to mere expansion. Many Americans became impatient of the chaos and saw, as did the philosopher Charles Peirce, that the community must control unbridled individualism. Slowly it dawned that there was danger in urban disorder and that America was not to be measured by bigness alone — art too must have its role. With much the same spirit and energy that they devoted to their business, Americans made amends for past errors. The City Beautiful movement was their offering. Without it we would not have had our great libraries, museums, terminals and civic centers, which captured the public imagination both here and abroad. It was the age in which the businessman made his greatest contribution to American culture and the government followed his lead.

1. PALACE AND MONUMENT

The new American millionaires may have been bold as brass in their titanic battles for control of business empires, but at first they were as timid of innovation as the less affluent when it came to adopting new forms of dwellings. True, the Potter Palmers built a stone turreted castle in Chicago which Boni de Castellane, the French dandy, called "sumptuous and abominable"; but when Marshall Field, the Chicago drygoods merchant, built himself a home on Prairie Avenue, a solid mansion of pressed brick and brownstone with a mansard roof, there was nothing in the building to show that Field was one of the wealthiest and most powerful men in the city. Alexander T. Stewart, his New York counterpart, had a larger mansion on Fifth Avenue, equally undistinguished. The standard was at last set by William Kissam Vanderbilt, grandson of the famous Commodore, who spent $3,000,000 between 1879 and 1881 on a house that once stood on the corner of 52nd Street and Fifth Avenue. Designed by Richard Morris Hunt, this building heralded the arrival of the private "palace."

How gay were the gala evenings when the house was ablaze with lights and Willie and I, crouching on hands and knees behind the balustrade of the musicians' gallery, looked on a festive scene below — the long dinner table covered with a damask cloth, a gold service and red roses, the lovely crystal and china, the grownups in their fine clothes [recalls Consuelo Vanderbilt Balsan, who, as Duchess of Marlborough, was afterwards to be the mistress of an older English palace].

The dining room was enormous and had at one end twin Renaissance mantel-pieces and on one side a huge stained-glass window, depicting the Field of the Cloth of Gold on which the kings of England and France were surrounded with their knights, all not more magnificently arrayed than the ladies a-glitter with jewels seated in high-backed tapestry chairs behind which stood footmen in knee breeches. Next to this big dining room was a small breakfast room adorned with Flemish tapestries and Rembrandt's portrait of the Turkish Chief. Then came a white drawing room hung with a fine set of Boucher tapestries; here were the beautiful lacquer *secrétaire* and commode, with bronzes chiseled by Gouthière, made for Marie Antoinette. Next door our living room, a paneled Renaissance salon, looked out on Fifth Avenue.

Despite the hours of tedium which must have passed in these rooms, where uneasy formality rivaled Spanish etiquette in its severity, what pleasure they gave to the innocent beholder and how significant was the patronage extended to the arts!

It is recorded in George Harvey's life of Henry Clay Frick that the Pittsburgher, already a Carnegie partner at the age of thirty-one, walking one day on Fifth Avenue with Andrew Mellon, the future Secretary of the Treasury, paused before Hunt's great mansion, still in process of construction, and speculated on the cost of its maintenance. This was in 1880, twenty-five years before Frick, having sold his holdings to United States Steel, himself moved to New York and rented one of the Vanderbilt mansions.

In 1914 Frick moved into his own palace, built for him by Carrère and Hastings at a cost of $5,400,000. This mansion, one of the last left on the avenue, now houses, as its builder planned, one of the world's most magnificent art collections, which Frick assembled and left to the public as a museum. We can

be thankful for this indulgence on the part of our millionaires, who were abetted by the architects and artists of the period. Witness the Havemeyer collection, now in the Metropolitan Museum of Art, assembled on the advice of Mary Cassatt, and Mrs. Jack Gardner's Italian palace on the Fenway in Boston, which John Singer Sargent and Bernard Berenson helped to fill with treasures.

Palace after palace rose on the great avenue, until by the 1900's it had become one of the sights of the nation, exciting the envy and admiration of all, and attacks on its extravagance from the nation's pulpits only served to make it seem more fascinating. For many a rising businessman and his wife it became an aim in life to have a Fifth Avenue address.

Limestone was the chief material of the Palace Era, varied occasionally by marble and travertine. Ornament was very carefully applied, both inside and out, and the taste of the furnishings was far superior to those of the houses built before 1880, more attention being given to the quality of the furniture and particularly painting. Sometimes artists like Augustus Saint-Gaudens and John La Farge were called in to contribute their skill. Hunt's palace style followed the style of the Francis I period in France, and it remained the fashion for a while, until in the late 1890's taste turned to the French Classic of Louis XV and Louis XVI.

Only a few examples of the private palace can be seen in New York today, but many are still to be found in Newport, Rhode Island, where rich New Yorkers summered in large numbers. It was the heyday of the resort. Here Hunt built "Ochre Court" in 1888 for Ogden Goelet, whose fortune in New York City real estate permitted him this extravagance. Hunt also designed the classical "Marble

House" for William Kissam Vanderbilt in 1892 and, three years later, the famous "Breakers" for Cornelius Vanderbilt II, today opened to the public for the benefit of the Newport Preservation Society by his daughter, the Countess Lâszló Széchényi. Horace Trumbauer, the Philadelphia architect, designed "The Elms" for the coal millionaire Edwin Berwind, a magnificent house in the Louis XV manner with sumptuous French interiors and gardens.

An error is often made today in believing that this love of splendor was confined to our millionaires, while the American people shunned displays of luxury. In many ways we are an extravagant people, although our extravagance may find its outlet in sports and clothes and all too rarely in the arts and the embellishing of our cities. The building of private palaces by the American rich was only one expression of the period. Hunt's design for the Vanderbilt house was the first signal of the change, but it was soon followed by others. McKim, Mead and White, between 1886 and 1896, built the great public library in Boston, a building inspired by the work of Leon Battista Alberti and of Henri Labrouste. With its murals by Puvis de Chavannes and its handsome marble hall and stairs it is one of the great buildings of the country.

These were signs of a new taste, to be sure, although the public was not fully aware of it. Other monuments stirred America's heart. On a bitter December day in 1884, President Chester A. Arthur watched the aluminum cap raised to the top of the Washington Monument, an event announcing its completion after thirty years and more of work. In the beautiful classical shaft America raised the highest masonry structure ever built by man. Two years later the Statue of Liberty by Bartholdi, with its base by

Hunt, lifted high her torch beside "the golden door" of New York Harbor. "We shall not forget that liberty has here made her home," was President Cleveland's welcome to the munificent gift of the French people to America, "nor shall her chosen altar be neglected." Emma Lazarus sang her beautiful song to the New Colossus: "Give me your tired, your poor, Your huddled masses yearning to breathe free . . ." Americans now had two spectacular monuments, which could only find comparison far back in history in the days of Hellenistic Greece and Imperial Rome.

A third appeared in 1889, on the centenary of Washington's inauguration in New York. In homage, President Harrison, imitating the first President, went by boat from Elizabethport, New Jersey, to the foot of Wall Street across a harbor where "small boats with double-reefed sails and beer ballast were under your bow every moment" and "ferryboats, river boats, tugs, yachts and launches were stepping on each other's heels, climbing each other's backs and kicking each other's elbows . . ." On the edge of Washington Square the President was greeted by a large temporary arch by Stanford White, the first elaborate arch since those built for Lafayette sixty-five years before. New Yorkers were so enthusiastic about White's creation that they subscribed to build a permanent one, the stone arch now standing in the square at the end of Fifth Avenue, the first permanent arch of triumph in America. The Washington Monument, the Statue of Liberty and the Washington Arch were symbols of a new power and a new yearning on the part of the American people.

In the Statue of Liberty could be seen more than the figure of Liberty holding high her light of Freedom, more than the symbol of friendship between the two great republics. The new colossus stood for the joining of the two nations in the classical tradition. American artists and architects had now begun to study in France. The only architectural school of any tradition and distinction in the world at the time was in Paris. To the Ecole Nationale Supérieure des Beaux-Arts streamed the students, who, at the expense of the French government, for there was no tuition fee, obtained a first-class education. After three or four years abroad, they were at home in at least one foreign language and they had at their fingertips the great examples of world art from Edinburgh to Istanbul. Louis Sullivan, although he spent a good part of his life battling the classical tradition, freely acknowledged his debt to France. The Ecole opened his eyes, he wrote in *The Autobiography of an Idea*, "to the quality and reach of French thought; to its richness, its firmness, its solidity, above all, the severity of its discipline beneath so smooth a surface." Knowledge and discipline were the French lessons for American artists, especially the architects, and they came back to create a style that, as Fiske Kimball has pointed out, had no equal anywhere at the time, not even in France itself.

At first, it is true, many of the protagonists of the classical returned from France under the archaeological influence of Viollet-le-Duc, an enemy of the Ecole. The two leaders of Picturesque Secessionism, Richardson and Sullivan, were students of the famous school, but many of the men who were accused of being under its influence had never set foot inside the doors. Neither Daniel H. Burnham nor Stanford White attended it. White, after several years in Richardson's office, discovered the classical on a trip through France with Charles Follen McKim and Augustus Saint-Gaudens.

A lesson of the Ecole des Beaux-Arts and, for that matter, of Europe, had been the value of the past. One of the first steps McKim took on leaving the Ecole was to explore our own past by touring New England in 1877 with his future partners, Stanford White and William Rutherford Mead. While Picturesque Secessionism was being acclaimed by fashion after the Centennial Exposition in Philadelphia, they came upon the neglected American Baroque. The revival of the American Baroque (which is still with us in the form of the Colonial Revival Style) stems from that trip. Almost at once Americans began to build in the tradition of their ancestors.

2. THE AMERICAN RENAISSANCE

The private palaces, the colossal monuments and the discovery of the American Baroque were milestones along the road to a new taste. Suddenly a vision appeared on the shores of Lake Michigan, springing full-blown like a sudden summer flower. The public rubbed its eyes and came in thousands. Flags waved in the hot midwestern sun, the air was filled with the rush of water from fountains and the murmur of admiring crowds; the vast white buildings were reflected in the giant basin, together with the great statue of the Republic; the monumental peristyle enclosed the Court of Honor and beyond there was a glimpse of the blue Lake Michigan and "the shadow of the dome of pleasure floated midway on the waves . . ." Such was the World's Columbian Exposition of 1893, Chicago's boast to all that, here on the prairie beside the inland sea, had risen an American forum filled with public palaces, rich with ornament and sculpture, to rival even ancient Rome. Some mocked the pretension at the time, and many have mocked it since; yet this temporary world of staff and plaster changed the taste of a nation.

One discerning critic came and left, only to return again, so overwhelmed was he by the spectacle. To Henry Adams "Paris had never approached" such a scene. "Was the American made to seem at home in it? Honestly, he has the air of enjoying it as though it were all his own," runs a passage in *The Education of Henry Adams.* "He felt it was good; he was proud of it; for the most part he acted as though he had passed his life in landscape gardening and architectural decorating." And Adams, recognizing the public taste for this new magnificence, insisted that "Chicago was the first expression of American thought as a unity; one must start there."

The Fair, which was so impressive to Adams and to countless others, has been much condemned, even more than the business age that created it. While the businessmen of the Gilded Age are at present being recognized as the great, if ruthless, organizers of the American Way of Life, their architects, sculptors, painters, landscape architects and city planners are still offered to us as bumbling imitators trained in a French school, who by turning to the tradition of the American Baroque and the American Roman crushed the flower of American art represented by Picturesque Secessionism. If we are now taking a more reasoned view of Rockefeller, Morgan and Harriman, might we not do the same for Burnham, McKim, Saint-Gaudens, Olmsted and the others who participated in designing the Fair and recognize them once and for all as great American artists?

The fascinating story of the Fair has yet to be told in all detail. The initiative of the Chicago businessmen was only the first step. Their master stroke was re-

taining Frederick Law Olmsted and Daniel H. Burnham among their consultants. To Olmsted belongs the design of the ground plan, to Burnham the unity of the whole and the responsibility for inviting the leading architects, sculptors and painters of the day to join in its creation. Hunt, Saint-Gaudens, McKim and Francis Millet, to name the most prominent, were among them. The co-operating architects unanimously chose the classical tradition for the architecture and decided on a uniform cornice line for the buildings on the Court of Honor. Like Jefferson they turned to the architecture of the ancients, because it had "the approbation of thousands of years..." Or as one of them, Henry Van Brunt of Kansas City, put it, they looked to "a uniform and ceremonious style – a style evolved from and expressive of the highest civilization in history" and not "a medieval or any other form of romantic, archeological or picturesque art."

Their triumph stemmed from three conditions: unity of plan, unity of architecture and magnitude. To these a fourth must be added, collaboration among all the arts. The return to the great classical tradition was well launched. So that when Burnham announced, "There are two sorts of architectural beauty, first, that of an individual building; and second, that of an orderly and fitting arrangement of many buildings; the relationship of all the buildings is more important than anything else," the concept may have been unheard of in American architecture and city planning since the time of Ramée and Jefferson; but the seed fell on cultivated ground.

It is true that a thin thread of government patronage had continued even through the Age of Steam and Iron. While the Picturesque was very much in vogue, the federal government itself had maintained the standards of the American Roman or Federal Style. In 1855 Constantino Brumidi began his herculean work of decorating the Capitol with frescoes. This humble Italian artist, who was driven from his homeland because of his republican principles, completed in 1865 the great "Apotheosis of Washington" which fills the dome. He was then sixty years old. He died fourteen years later, still at work on the frieze; only recently has he received just recognition for his handiwork, thanks to his biographer, Mrs. John R. Murdock. At the mid-century, too, Ammi Burnham Young, now a forgotten architect, succeeded Robert Mills as architect to the Treasury Department (it was in 1852) and from his drawing board came a number of post offices and custom houses, many of them to be found still throughout the country. Best remembered for his designs of the Vermont capitol at Montpelier and the Boston Custom House, Young's government buildings in Portland, Maine, Providence, Rhode Island, Galveston, Texas, and Galena, Illinois, command attention by their beautiful proportions and the classical restraint exercised by this most Roman of American architects.

With the passage of the Tarsney Act in 1893 Congress renewed the tradition of patronage by authorizing the Secretary of the Treasury to obtain designs for public buildings by competition among the leaders of the architectural profession. A fixed fee of 6 per cent of the construction cost was the reward for the winner of the competition. By this law the federal government gave architecture official recognition as an art essential to the community; with the best talent of the country at its disposal government patronage of architecture was soon reflected in the quality of its buildings. (Unfortunately in 1912 a later Congress, under the constant pressure of economy drives, repealed the act, but not before such buildings as the New York Custom House by Cass Gilbert were completed.)

Local governments followed suit with a lively interest in better architecture. One new state capitol arose after the other, especially in the West. Cass Gilbert did the designs for the Minnesota capitol in St. Paul in 1896, and the Arkansas capitol in Little Rock in 1899. The Rhode Island capitol (1895–1901) belongs to McKim, Mead and White; George B. Post and Sons designed Wisconsin's (1906–17) in Madison. One of the more powerful works was the Pennsylvania capitol (1904–6) in Harrisburg by Joseph M. Huston; it is distinguished for its murals by Edwin Austin Abbey and the sculptured groups of George Gray Barnard. In Jefferson City the Missouri capitol, completed by Tracy and Swartout in 1917, stands out as perhaps the most Roman of all in scale and character. Despite one or two failures these capitols are magnificent and nowhere more so than in their interiors, where embellishments abound and where all the arts have found a place. In our own time bareness and function have been the chief architectural preoccupation, but these domed capitols invite Americans to the visual splendors of gold and marble not found in the newer state office buildings, or indeed, in any modern government buildings today.

Coinciding with the new interest in monuments and public buildings, the time had come to improve the home of the federal government. L'Enfant's work in Washington, after the initial efforts, had fallen into neglect. The Romantic Revival had invaded the capital city with the Gothic Smithsonian Institution and the Age of Steam and Iron had run a railroad across the Mall. After serving as warehouse and hospital during the Civil War, the federal city was a shambles. The Capitol, "a splendid building, unfolds its repeated colonnades and uplifts its isolated dome at the end of a long vista of saloons and tobacco shops," Henry James noted at the time.

The American people, disregarding Spencerian individualism, were determined that art should bring order to the national capital. The first move was the revival of the L'Enfant plan by the McMillan Commission in 1901. Forty years or so earlier an attempt had been made to create a supervising committee to improve the city on the petition of a group of artists to President Buchanan and Congress, but nothing came of the move. Then in the time of Theodore Roosevelt, Senator James McMillan of Michigan appointed a subcommittee to the senate committee on the District of Columbia, naming as members Burnham, McKim, Saint-Gaudens and Olmsted. The Washington we see before us today is the result of their work.

They studied the L'Enfant plan, then went abroad to see what the past had to offer and, on their return, incorporated improvements to L'Enfant's work in the plan of 1901. The restoration of the Mall was first on their list; next came the location of new public buildings, and then memorials, new and old, were related to a general pattern of improvement. Further, the parks were systematized and joined. It was Burnham who persuaded Alexander Cassatt, president of the Pennsylvania Railroad, to remove the station from the Mall. The architect suggested a new location south of it, but Cassatt, improving on his idea, and in cooperation with the Baltimore and Ohio Railroad, agreed to build the Union Station

where it now stands, well to the north. The heart of Washington was thus restored approximately to the original scheme of the 1790's.

In 1910 on the motion of Senator Elihu Root a National Commission of Fine Arts with seven members was created to advise on and approve future developments in the District of Columbia. President Theodore Roosevelt explained to the American Institute of Architects how it functioned:

Whenever hereafter a public building is provided for, it should be erected in accordance with a carefully thought-out plan adopted long before . . . it should not only be beautiful in itself, but fitting in its relations to the whole scheme of the public buildings, the parks and the drives of the District.

What had begun as part of the training in an atelier of the Ecole des Beaux-Arts in Paris, and then found temporary form in Chicago in 1893, now achieved permanence in the national capital. From Bangor, Maine, to San Diego, California, every city and town attempted self-improvement. Among the first was Greater Boston, which in 1893 created its Metropolitan Park Commission for the central city and its surrounding communities. In that year Boston could count only 1900 acres of park lands as its own; ten years later Greater Boston had more than 13,000 acres of park and 19 miles of ocean shore reserved for the public. Kansas City also began its improvements at the same time by creating a system of parks and boulevards. The improvements in St. Louis stemmed from its 1904 exposition, when the Art Museum, the only permanent building of the fair, was made the focal point for the development of Forest Park. In Cedar Rapids, Iowa, the first suggestions for improvement were offered in 1901 by the city's Commercial

Club, which directed attention to the shore development of the Cedar River. A River-front Improvement Commission was appointed a year later and in the following fifteen years the whole central portion of the city was changed to an elegant vista of bridges and esplanades. Des Moines, the capital of the state, effected much the same transformation to its waterfront on the initiative of its Civic Improvement and Town Planning Committees. Along with new park systems and waterfronts came the civic centers. The new capitol buildings and town halls would have been ridiculous without civic design. Typical of the changes was the removal of the telephone wires and poles from State Street in Madison, Wisconsin, giving the new domed capitol the approach that was its due. In Harrisburg a similar awakening took place at the turn of the century, and with the completion of the great Pennsylvania capitol other work was pushed. A civic center was planned by the state and the city around the capitol building in 1917 and carried to completion in the twenty years that followed.

Art museums and libraries were built by the score in the City Beautiful period. In 1898 it was decided to consolidate several of New York's privately-endowed public library foundations into one. Among these were the Astor Library, given by John Jacob Astor, and the Tilden Foundation, left by Samuel J. Tilden, Democratic candidate for the Presidency in 1876. A competition was held for a new building to bring them together. Carrère and Hastings won, and the great structure, which is one of the city's best-known institutions, was completed in 1911. Hastings was also responsible for the design for the beautiful bronze bases of the two flagpoles that stand before it. They were executed by Raffaele J. Men-

coni and were cast in the famous Tiffany Studios. Buffalo obtained its handsome Albright Art Gallery, the work of Green and Wicks, in 1905, and many other cities housed their art collections in handsome galleries on the wave of the new interest in the arts.

Church architecture broke away from the influence of Richardson, and although many new churches were built, relatively few were carried out in the classical tradition. In general the fervent Gothicist Ralph Adams Cram had his way. Preaching Gothic as the only true Christian architecture this latter-day medievalist won many patrons of all sects. To him and his partners Goodhue and Ferguson, we owe the sumptuous St. Thomas's (1908) in New York, the First Baptist (1909) in Pittsburgh and the Fourth Presbyterian (1912) in Chicago. It was the distinction of the church architecture of the period that the evangelical Protestant joined the Episcopal and the Roman Catholic in building decorated houses of worship. (Cram, Goodhue and Ferguson's most outstanding work was the imposing addition, including the chapel, to the United States Military Academy at West Point in 1904.)

The college campus, too, went through a metamorphosis as the Grand Design returned to the "academical village." If we compare Olmsted and Vaux's plan for Berkeley and the University of California (1866) with the former's plan for Leland Stanford Junior University (1888), the change is astonishing. The first is Downingesque and the second extremely formal. The later plan for the University of California campus (1902) by Emile Bénard and John Galen Howard is in the best classical manner. With the tremendous expansion of American universities many classical campuses were built at this time. The American garden, like the campus, also changed. Largely due to the influence of Charles Adams Platt and Edith Wharton, the Italian garden came to America. One of Platt's best gardens, although neglected, is that of the Harold R. McCormick estate in Lake Forest. The best known example of his influence is Meridian Hill Park in Washington, familiar to music lovers because of its summer concerts. The French formal garden also enjoyed a considerable vogue, and although many of the great ones have gone before the omnivorous subdivider, one or two of those of Jacques Gréber and the younger Olmsted can still be found on the Atlantic seaboard at Newport, on Long Island and in the environs of Philadelphia.

To round out the pageantry of the age came the pyrotechnician. Fireworks abounded on every occasion, public and private. America even had its own celebrated family of pyrotechnical artists, the Pains. Among the many who attended their displays was Theodore Roosevelt, who, it is reported, "couldn't keep his hands off the stuff."

Even the staid railroad corporations were infected by the rage for display. Instead of the smoky depots of the Age of Steam and Iron beautiful stations sheltered the waiting passengers, and the city, which until now had been knocked about by the railroad, had a new embellishment. Burnham built more than one great station; his Pennsylvania Railroad Terminal in Pittsburgh has a waiting room where gold, a form of ornament too rarely used in the United States, forms part of the decoration. Alexander Cassatt, on a visit to his famous sister, the painter Mary Cassatt living outside Paris, had seen how the Paris-Orléans Railroad had electrified its tracks into the French capital, and he was determined that the Pennsylvania Railroad should have its own station in New York. Electrification

proved the solution, and in 1906 he commissioned McKim, Mead and White to build the monumental Pennsylvania Station. The New York Central followed suit after electrifying its lines. It retained the architects Reed and Stem and Warren and Wetmore to do the Grand Central. In no small part due to the skillful engineering of Colonel William Wilgus, who devised the method of routing the trains underground, the station is one of the handsomest and most convenient in the world.

In spite of the inevitable unevenness of execution, all of these buildings, even the modest libraries made possible by the philanthropy of Andrew Carnegie, have a character that reveals the stylistic aspirations of the age. This style was in a recognizable classical tradition, essentially a public style, to be embellished by all the arts and to be judged by all the people. "When you get through with your work on the other side and come home to build," wrote McKim in 1909 to Lawrence Grant White, the son of his deceased partner, "you will find opportunities awaiting that no other country has offered in modern times. The scale is Roman and it will have to be sustained."

The age of the City Beautiful was one in which architect-planners dominated. The reward of the architects for first visualizing the City Beautiful in America was the commission to build it. The initiative for improvement came from business and professional groups, and among their fellows the architects and the landscape architects assumed the lead. In every city where there was a chapter of the American Institute of Architects, designs, pamphlets and detailed reports poured forth.

The greatest rewards were reserved for the most prominent of all architect-planners, Daniel H. Burnham. In addition to work at the Chicago World's Fair and in Washington, he did plans for Cleveland, San Francisco (in association with Edward H. Bennett) and Manila in the Philippine Islands. Although his important practice carried him to all parts of the country, the improvement of Chicago was always the great aim of his life. In 1897 he had told the Merchants' Club "that the time has come for Chicago to make herself attractive" and he outlined a number of suggestions. Nothing came of them. Undiscouraged he kept advancing ideas for improvement, for he always believed that the city should be a place "for men and women to live and for children to grow up in; his chief idea was to make conditions for working healthy and agreeable, and facilities for recreation both abundant and available." Then in 1906 the Commercial Club of Chicago invited him to prepare a comprehensive plan of the city. In the next three years he devoted himself with the assistance of a large staff to the preparation of the plan, a labor of love on his part for he accepted no remuneration for any of his city plans. The unusual aspect of Burnham's plan was its extent. For one thing, he did not confine planning to the city but carried it to the region beyond. Secondly, he took into consideration railroads, highways, parks, playgrounds, forests and bathing beaches. And a third distinction was the dramatization of the architectural effect possible in skillful planning. At the center he wanted low buildings dominated by the high dome of the city hall; tall buildings would form the outer rim. The plan was magnificently presented to the public by the Commercial Club in the form of a handsome book, the first comprehensive plan for an American city of regional scope and authority. The Wacker Manual, a simplified account of the plan, was later printed in the thousands and used as a textbook in Chicago's schools.

No plan has ever influenced an American city in quite the same way that Burnham's dream captured the imagination of Chicago. Even in the corrupt regime of Mayor "Big Bill" Thompson, its suggested improvements were pushed ahead. The new lakefront, the widening of Michigan Avenue, the creation of the Cook County Forest Reserve and the Wacker Drive are the better known improvements that eventually resulted. Very unfortunately, Burnham's plan for a civic center was not realized and the city is still without one. For all the spread of city planning since, it is a compliment to Burnham's genius that the plan has not yet found its equal, even in the well-known Regional Plan of 1929 for New York City, which dwelt inevitably on administration, engineering and legal problems. The times were changing and there were signs that other matters would occupy the American people. The automobile, until then a sign of wealth, was about to become available to all; Henry Ford made his first Model T in the year that Burnham's plan was published. The well-to-do who were deserting the city for their suburban arcadias were soon to forget the other nine tenths who remained in the center, where the City Efficient was to obscure the importance of the City Beautiful.

Before we leave the American Renaissance, which wrought such a profound change in American architecture as in all the arts, we would do well to recall the famous words of Burnham to city planners, written shortly before his death in 1912.

Make no little plans; they have no magic to stir men's blood and probably themselves will not be realized. Make big plans; aim high in hope and work, remembering that a noble, logical diagram once recorded will never die, but long after we are gone will be a living thing, asserting itself with ever-growing insistency. Remember that our sons and our grandsons are going to do things that would stagger us. Let your watchword be order and your beacon beauty.

Valete, ac plaudite — those words will forever be remembered in the city to which a man of vision brought the blessings of civic design and by generations of American city dwellers yet to come.

Roy Lubove: PROGRESSIVISM, PLANNING AND HOUSING

Although the city still challenges planners and architects, the initial impetus for planning, zoning, and beautification came in the late nineteenth century. In a chapter from his book, The Progressives and the Slums, *Roy Lubove discusses early attempts to improve housing and enact zoning laws.*

And when the heavens rolled away and St. John beheld the new Jerusalem, so a new vision of a new London, a new Washington, Chicago, or New York breaks with the morning's sunshine upon the degradation, discomfort, and baseness of modern city life. There are born a new dream and a new hope.

CHARLES M. ROBINSON,
Modern Civic Art, 1918

THE initial spur to city planning in the United States came from the spectacular Chicago Fair of 1893. Chicago's "White City" has been aptly described as "a laboratory — a testing ground — not only for the problems of civic design but also for determining the best hygienic and protective methods for urban application." Thanks to the skill of its chief architect, Daniel H. Burnham, and landscape architect, Frederick Law Olmsted, the planned unity and classic dignity of the Fair became for Americans "a revelation" and "a benediction." Here, for the first time, they glimpsed "what an ideal city might be."

The Fair did not represent simply an experiment in civic art and architecture. Its organizers faced many practical problems: police and fire protection, the creation of water, sewerage, and transportation systems, the provision of cultural and recreational facilities. The Columbian Exposition suggested that the aesthetic and utilitarian could be coordinated to produce a higher form of urban civilization. That "glorious fairy city which sprung up almost overnight in Jackson Park, in Chicago" was America's hope and promise of what the twentieth-century city might be.

The classic facade of the White City has been criticized by some, notably Lewis Mumford, as a dubious contribution to

From Roy Lubove, *The Progressive and the Slums: Tenement House Reform in New York City, 1890–1917* (Pittsburgh: University of Pittsburgh Press, 1962), pp. 217–238, 244–245. Reprinted by permission of the University of Pittsburgh Press.

America's architectural and civic development. The architects had "chanted a Roman litany above the Babel of individual styles." The World's Fair triumph had "suggested to the civic enthusiast that every city might become a fair: it introduced the notion of the City Beautiful as a sort of municipal cosmetic." Mumford's savage critique has validity. It is true that the classic vogue in architecture and the City Beautiful concept in civic design which sprang from the Fair had certain baneful consequences. The Fair, however, performed one valuable service which could excuse many faults; it planted the seed basic to the art and science of city planning. From the Exposition came the realization that a city is an organism of interrelated, interdependent parts whose efficiency depends upon planned and orderly growth.

The dominating quality of the Exposition, that which made the most lasting impression upon spectators, was its unity. "It remained for Chicago," the president of the American Civic Association observed, "to awaken our dormant sense of form and appropriateness in architecture and environment, and to show what planning could accomplish." Never before, affirmed a contemporary, "was the unity of a single design so triumphant." The lesson of the Fair was the dependence of the city upon "proportion, balance, and ordered suitability of parts." However one might disparage the somewhat sterile classicism of the Fair, its ultimate influence was salutary. In contrast to the typically ugly, sprawling, squalid American industrial city of the nineteenth century, the White City was a beatific vision of blue lagoons, luxurious green lawns, and monumental splendor. Americans saw in its planned beauty, order and picturesque design an irresistible alternative to the dirt, monotony and pervading dinginess of their existing municipalities.

This was the real meaning of the Chicago Fair; it created new ideals and standards by which to measure the quality of urban life.

Until about 1909 the City Beautiful was the principal expression of the newly discovered passion for planned civic growth. Cities hired architects to produce elaborate schemes for civic centers, tree-lined boulevards in the European manner, parks, and a variety of other forms of ornamentation: public art, plant decoration, sculpture, street signs, even lamp posts. The City Beautiful also included several negative ideals, such as noise abatement and the control of street advertising.

Besides Daniel H. Burnham, the chief exponent of the City Beautiful for many years was Charles Mulford Robinson, a Rochester, New York, architect. A prolific author, Robinson labored to convert "the spirit of aesthetic renaissance," "civic art's transforming touch," into a secular municipal religion. For Robinson the City Beautiful was not merely an aesthete's delight, a genteel pastime, but an inspired social vision: "The moral and spiritual standards of the people will be advanced by this art, and their political ideals will rise with a civic pride and a community spirit born of the appreciation that they are citizens of 'no mean city.'" The tenement population, particularly, would benefit from the sensual delights of the City Beautiful: ". . . to make the homes not only livable but attractive, to awaken ambition, to encourage the life of the beautiful — would not this, this glorious aggregate, be the first task that civic art would undertake?" Robinson and other exponents of the City Beautiful interpreted civic art much as Jacob Riis interpreted nature; it was a moral force able to elevate the character and ideals of those touched by its magic wand.

In time the almost exclusive dominion

of the City Beautiful was challenged. After 1909 the "City Useful" overtook, then surpassed the City Beautiful in the theoretical formulations of city planners, if not always in their actual plans. The desire for urban unity and harmony aroused by the Chicago Fair achieved a more mature expression in the new utilitarian-oriented planning movement.

There were several reasons for the new point of view. The City Beautiful was a narrow and pathetically fragile ideal, remote from business, commerce, industry, transportation, poverty, and similar mundane but integral features of urban life. Once the glow of the White City had dimmed, the need to incorporate these features into a planning scheme became apparent. In addition, new men who achieved prominence in planning insisted that the City Beautiful must be subordinate to the City Useful if the goal of "a better, more orderly, more livable city" was to be attained. Conspicuous among the champions of utilitarian planning was John Nolen, a Massachusetts landscape architect and founding father of modern planning in America. Very different from Robinson's ideal was the social and practical emphasis of Nolen. The absence of beauty troubled him less than the faulty street arrangement, the condition of the waterfronts, the uncoordinated transportation system, the "unsanitary and demoralizing influences of slums." If housing reform in the broadest sense signified the belief that the health and welfare of the people in an urban-industrial society were too important to remain in the hands of the entrepreneur exclusively, the utilitarian-minded city planning movement after 1909 evolved from the conviction that urban growth in general was too important to continue unplanned and uncoordinated, the product of countless shortsighted and selfish private decisions.

2

Most significant in explaining the character of the planning movement after 1909, particularly in relation to housing, were two European developments. The City Beautiful remained dominant until planners and housing reformers had digested the implications of the garden city in England and the zoning program in Germany. The garden city was the product of a book by an obscure court stenographer named Ebenezer Howard; and Germany's zoning legislation unfolded from the experiments of Franz Adickes, Bürgermeister of Altona, a Hamburg suburb, and then of Frankfurt-am-Main. The concept of the garden city and zoning equipped American planners, for the first time, with a concrete formula for urban reconstruction based upon dispersion of population and industry.

In his book *Tomorrow* (1898), Howard proposed an alternative to city or country life possessing the advantages of both, but none of their inconveniences. The alternative would be a magnet, producing the "spontaneous movement" of people from crowded cities to the country. "Town and country *must be married*," Howard affirmed, for out of the union would "spring a new hope, a new life, a new civilization."

Howard outlined a plan for a garden city limited in population to about 32,000. Neither the first nor future garden cities would expand beyond that size, for any excess population would simply serve as the nucleus for an entirely new community. Each garden city would be surrounded forever by an agricultural belt producing food for the community and preventing suburban sprawl. Howard located factories, warehouses, and other business establishments in the outer ring of his circular city, separated from the people's homes in the inner circle. Besides homes, the inner circle would include attractive radial boulevards, parks, and civic, cultural, and shopping facilities.

Garden city was to be governed by a central council composed of the officers of various departments elected by the inhabitants. Its revenues depended entirely upon rents. Since the community as a whole owned the land, any increase in its value would revert back to the people. Thus no "unearned increment" would flow into the pockets of landlords and speculators as a consequence of the community's growth and prosperity.

A year after Howard's book appeared, a Garden City Association in England was formed to promote the plan. Its efforts resulted in 1903 in the formation of the First Garden City, Ltd., which purchased and developed on garden city principles a 4,000-acre estate at Letchworth. Letchworth suggested to planners and housing reformers in America and Europe that garden city was no idle, impractical dream fit only for a small cult of enthusiasts. It was a financial and social success.

Garden city's appeal to reformers in England and America is not difficult to explain. On paper, at least, it was a simple scheme. One had only to grasp a few elementary principles, locate a site, and gather sufficient funds to purchase and develop it. The cooperative benefits of garden city impressed a generation of municipal reformers who attributed many of the evils of urban life to unsocialized individualism and private greed. Here at last was a way to insure that landed wealth created by the community would return to its source to benefit all the people instead of a few monopolists. At the same time, however, there was plenty of scope for private initiative in the agricultural, industrial, and retail trades integral to garden city's economy. The balance between industry and agriculture in Howard's machine-age utopia particularly interested a generation which feared that man was losing touch with nature, stifling himself in the smoke and soot of the great industrial city. Finally, garden city was influential as a thoroughly planned community. In contrast to Chicago's White City, an ephemeral fairyland meant to vanish when the Fair had ended, people actually lived and worked there. It was the most concrete example of the potentialities inherent in city planning for creating a new civilization.

Certain features of the garden city plan particularly impressed housing reformers. The limitations on population and the number of houses per acre seemed an ideal system for preventing the congestion out of which the slum had evolved. Equally important, the garden city program, revolutionary in principle but conservative in method, could be used against existing slums. It did not involve expensive and confiscatory slum clearance schemes in the core of the city where congestion had inflated land and property values. If enough of the urban population could be removed to garden cities, the inflated structure of values would collapse of its own weight. Land would become cheap enough to house people comfortably again, even in the heart of the city.

Although the garden city was the ideal goal, two modifications of its principles received even greater attention from planners and housing reformers in America. The garden suburb and garden village involved the identical end of urban decentralization, but were less ambitious in scope and thus were better suited for immediate application. The garden suburb was a planned residential community on the outskirts of a city. Although it was only an appendage which lacked the self-sufficiency of garden city, it seemed a practical way to house a sizeable percentage of the urban working population in attractive surroundings. The inspiration for the garden suburb also derived from England, where it formed a part of the great cooperative movement. In 1901 the Ealing Tenants, Ltd. had been formed by a group of cooperators to develop a suburban residential estate. Their success resulted in the organization of similar associations in English cities. The Co-Partnership Tenant's Council provided central leadership as an organizing and propagandizing agency; the associations themselves were affiliated in the Co-Partnership Tenants, Ltd. of London. By 1909 workers' cooperative associations owned almost $40,000,000 worth of property.

There was also a middle road between the self-sufficiency of the garden city and the strictly residential character of the garden suburb. The garden village was a residential community organized around one or a few industries. The influence of two of the English garden villages upon planners and housing reformers in the Progressive era cannot be overestimated. In Port Sunlight and Bournville they saw a brilliant alternative to the evils of crowded city life. Port Sunlight, a garden village located outside Liverpool, was founded by Sir William Lever, the soap manufacturer. Here was a planned community of winding, tree-lined roads, spacious parks, and handsome cottages with gardens. Lever operated the village for his employees at a loss, but found recompense in their contentment and good health. Observers were usually charmed by what they saw at Port Sunlight. One of them, prior to a visit, "had not known that there was anywhere in the world a village in which there was nowhere to be found one ugly, inartistic, unsanitary, or other demoralizing feature."

Bournville was also an industrial village founded by a benevolent employer. It was developed as a model community after 1895 by George Cadbury, the cocoa manufacturer. In 1900 Cadbury turned over the property, located outside Birmingham, in trust to the nation. Besides its spacious, well-designed cottages, Bournville displayed such amenities as a meeting house; an institute containing a library, lecture hall, classrooms and similar facilities; children's playgrounds; wooded areas and village greens. According to Bournville's architect, it was the village of the future, "a village of healthy homes and pleasant surroundings, where fresh air is abundant and beauty present."

After the inspiring examples of Port Sunlight and Bournville had permeated the thinking of American planners and housing reformers, they discovered that America actually had a tradition of industrial villages. Unfortunately, many of them were mining and cotton-mill towns, merely squalid caricatures of the English prototypes in physical layout and management. Not even the best specimens of the American industrial village, such as Pullman, Illinois, could compare with Port Sunlight or Bournville in the quality of planning or the benefits conferred upon their inhabitants.

Nonetheless, housing reformers were optimistic about the future of the industrial village. In model garden villages detached or row cottages, limited in number per acre, would provide excellent housing in contrast to the dreary flats or tenements to which so many workers were accustomed. The garden village was practical, for industrialists would surely find a contented and healthy working force to their advantage, not to mention the low taxes and land prices of suburban locations. It was not necessary or even desirable for a company to build and manage an industrial village. The work could be delegated to a subsidiary company or to private developers subject to strict standards of planning and design. In any case, the company must avoid both the paternalism which created resentment at Pullman and the despotism of most mining and cotton-mill towns.

A number of planned or semi-planned industrial suburbs had appeared before World War I. Gary, Indiana, one of the largest, showed little evidence of planning or the social responsibility reformers hoped to stimulate among companies engaged in real estate operations. Within three years (1906–9), the United States Steel Corporation transformed marshland and sand dunes into a city of 12,000 equipped with paved streets, sidewalks, utilities, public schools, shops and residences; but since the Corporation had been more interested in expanding its steel production than in city-building it did not employ planners and it acquiesced in the speculative development of homes by private realtors on land south of the Wabash Railroad tracks. Hundreds of box-shaped, frame houses sprang up for unskilled workers, and no housing codes interfered with the builders.

More satisfactory specimens of industrial suburbs encouraged reformers to retain faith in the garden village. The Goodyear Tire and Rubber Company organized a subsidiary in 1912, which hired the landscape architect Warren H. Manning to develop a 100-acre tract adjoining Akron, Ohio. About 250 brick and stucco homes of five to eight rooms had been erected by 1916 and sold to employees. Similarly, the Norton Grinding Company of Worcester, Massachusetts, commissioned Grosvenor Atterbury to develop a ninety-acre site. Under Atterbury's supervision, the Company built some sixty detached and semi-detached frame and stucco houses. John Nolen, a fervid champion of industrial housing, planned a garden village at Kistler, Pennsylvania, for the Mount Union Refractories Company. Nolen's plans for the fifty-acre tract included parks, playgrounds, and a school.

Emile Perrot, a Philadelphia architect familiar with the English garden village, helped plan Marcus Hook near Chester, Pennsylvania, for the Viscose Company. The Marcus Hook development included 215 brick row houses, a store, and a recreation building. Two additional experiments which aroused the interest of housing reformers were Morgan Park outside of Duluth, where the Minnesota Steel Company erected single-family detached and row houses for more than 400 families, and Eclipse Park, near Beloit, Wisconsin, where the Fairbank Morse Company built 350 detached houses for employees, ranging in price from $2,400 for four rooms to $3,100 for eight rooms.

No garden cities appeared in America, and reformers could claim an extremely limited success in promoting the garden village. With a few exceptions like the Homewood project of the City and Suburban Homes Company, reformers could refer only to Forest Hills Gardens in Long Island to illustrate the planned garden suburb in America. Designed by Frederick Law Olmsted, Jr., and Grosvenor Atterbury, Forest Hills Gardens was sponsored by the Russell Sage Foundation in 1909. Its Tudor-style homes with spacious lawns, network of winding roads, shopping center, small parks and public schools illustrated the virtues of large-scale comprehensive planning. Yet Forest Hills proved nothing except the obvious — that attractive suburban communities could be created for those able to afford them.

In a report which appeared in the United States Bureau of Labor Statistics

Monthly Review for November 1917, Leifur Magnusson examined 236 company housing projects. Few of the companies hired architects and planners of the caliber of Nolen, Atterbury, or Perrot. No American industrial communities matched Bournville or Port Sunlight, and many of them like Gary, or the mining towns of the Colorado Fuel and Iron Company, exhibited no housing or planning features worthy of emulation. For the reformer, however, the industrial village and garden suburb seemed in theory a promising alternative to the city tenement or flat. If only enough industrialists and philanthropists could be convinced of the economic and social advantages of the garden village and suburb, the reformer could strike at the heart of the housing problem by relieving the congestion of the industrial city. Here was a key point at which the housing and planning movements of the Progressive era intersected — relief of the congestion responsible for the tenement and slum through dispersion of work and population from the central city.

All Progressive housing reformers endorsed the garden city program or its modifications. Even Lawrence Veiller, the leading exponent of restrictive legislation, could not resist the allure of planned garden communities. Although Veiller observed that workers in most American industrial towns "live in squalid and sordid surroundings," in time, perhaps, "far-sighted employers of labor" might "develop their community in such a way that it will not only furnish a delightful dwelling place for their workers, but will be a real asset to the industry." Referring to the garden city, Veiller noted that by 1920 Letchworth contained eighty-two factories and workshops, 2,282 houses, and many shops and public buildings. It was a thriving community. England had

demonstrated to his satisfaction that "the Garden City is a practical scheme; of benefit to the workers, of benefit to industry, of benefit to the community, of benefit to the nation."

The COS Tenement House Committee promoted the garden city ideal and its variations whenever possible. It learned, for example, that Procter and Gamble was planning to establish a plant in Staten Island, and offered some free advice to William C. Procter. The Committee explained the merits of the industrial village, referring specifically to Port Sunlight, Bournville, and some American towns. It stressed its point by outlining the alternative to the planned, industrial village — the New York speculative tenement with its "increase in excessive drinking and gambling; overindulgence in all the dissipations which gain influence as the home ceases to be attractive; increase in crime, and decrease in reliability, intelligence, contentment and efficiency." Though nothing came of the Committee's proposal, it reflects the interest of the Progressive housing reformer in directing the flow of population and industry away from the congested core of the city and into the country.

3

The garden city program provided only for the planned development of new communities. It did not affect the expansion of existing municipalities or protect their better neighborhoods from future congestion. In zoning, housing reformers and planners thought they had found a device which would insure the orderly growth of existing cities. A planning weapon which had achieved maturity in Germany after 1900, zoning combined with the garden city movement after 1909 to enhance the utilitarian impulse superseding the City Beautiful.

Although businessmen would promote zoning mainly to protect their financial interests, reformers viewed it in the broader perspective of the general social welfare; zoning would improve urban housing and living conditions by controlling population distribution.

German municipalities in rapid succession adopted zoning or districting regulations after 1900 in order to regulate expansion outward from the old (often medieval) central city. The German zoning program consisted essentially of three series of restrictions over building development. First, the city was districted into specific use areas: residential, industrial, commercial, and mixed. In residential neighborhoods, protected against industrial or commercial invasion, property values would presumably remain stable because home owners were safeguarded against indiscriminate land use; property values would not fluctuate wildly, for speculators could not exploit the uncertainty and fears of home owners.

German zoning also involved the establishment of height districts. Building heights in designated areas were limited to a certain multiple of the street width. Height regulation had a dual purpose: it prevented congestion by limiting the number of people who could live or work in a particular area and simultaneously insured a minimum of light and air for all the structures. Height districting, in addition, protected property owners. A developer, for example, was prohibited from erecting a tall tenement in a neighborhood of one-family homes.

German zoning, finally, involved the creation of bulk or area restrictions. These regulated such items as court and yard sizes and the percentage of a lot which could be covered. Like height regulations, these area restrictions also insured a minimum of light and air for

commercial as well as residential structures, and reduced overcrowding by limiting the amount of land which developers could improve.

American housing reformers and planners believed they had found in zoning a tool with which to control land speculation, the fluctuation of property values and, above all, congestion. Indeed, American municipal reformers commonly assumed that if we imposed zoning regulations to prevent overcrowding, we would plug the fountain from which many of the physical and social evils of urban life flowed. No program of social betterment could achieve results unless "accompanied by a reasonably successful attempt to lessen the congestion of population which now exists."

4

The crusade to reduce urban congestion in the Progressive era was part of, but distinct from, the housing reform and planning movements. It enlisted the support of social reformers of all varieties, including those interested in land, taxation, and child welfare. In New York City it developed its own program and organization, and no discussion of housing or city planning is complete without some mention of the anti-congestion campaign.

Early in the winter of 1907 a group of New York social workers decided to form an association dedicated to the relief of congestion and to the stimulation of public interest in its causes, consequences, and remedies. This group, which included such distinguished settlement leaders as Mary K. Simkhovitch, Lillian D. Wald, and Gaylord S. White, as well as Florence Kelley of the National Consumers' League, organized the Committee on Congestion of Population in New York (CCP). The Committee appointed Benjamin C. Marsh as its secretary. Like Veiller, Marsh was a talented organizer and administrator, outspoken in his convictions and gifted with a quick, original mind. He differed from Veiller and de Forest, however, in his receptivity to economic reforms unacceptable to the more conservative New Yorkers. Marsh remembered that when he first came to New York, Veiller introduced him to de Forest, pointing out that Marsh was particularly interested in the land problem. According to Marsh, "Mr. de Forrest [sic] looked at me with the maddening tolerance of a wise old man for a well-intentioned young fool and said, 'If you touch the land problem in New York, you probably won't last here two years.'"

After graduating from Iowa's Grinnell College in 1898, Marsh served a short term as assistant state secretary for the YMCA, followed by courses in political economy at the University of Chicago. He spent two years raising funds for the Congregationalist Board of Commissioners for Foreign Missions, exploring America's industrial cities and observing firsthand the living conditions of the nation's workers. Distressed by the widespread misery he encountered, he decided to learn more. Marsh accepted a fellowship in 1902 at the University of Pennsylvania in order to study the "homeless man" under the direction of Professor Simon Patten, and left for Europe the following summer to examine the old world's system of control over the beggar and tramp. His background in social work soon qualified him for appointment as secretary of the Pennsylvania Society to Protect Children from Cruelty, and in 1907 he received the call from the newly organized CCP.

Under Marsh's direction the CCP quickly spread its influence in the fields of congestion relief, housing reform, and planning. He scored an early triumph with the organization of New York's first congestion exhibit. Held in the Museum of Natural History in March 1908, the exhibit was patterned after those which Lawrence Veiller had arranged for the COS on housing and tuberculosis. Exhibitors included the Tenement House Department, COS and AICP, City and Suburban Homes Company, National Consumers' League, New York Child Labor Committee, and other welfare and reform agencies. Marsh toured the premises with Governor Hughes, pointing out to him "the most striking features." The exhibit aroused considerable public interest, which the CCP exploited to induce the New York City legislature to authorize the creation of an official congestion commission.

The New York Congestion Commission, appointed by Mayor Gaynor in 1910 and including Benjamin Marsh as its secretary, published a lengthy report in 1911. This unique social document involved a comprehensive examination of the causes, consequences, and possible remedies for New York's oppressive overcrowding of land and people. It discovered that the population and density for all New York's boroughs had increased between 1900–10. In Manhattan, for example, the population had leaped from 1,850,000 to 2,321,000; the density per acre rose from 131.8 to 166.1. The Commission argued that "for a good standard of housing for unskilled wage earners the maximum value of land should not exceed 50 cents per square foot." Land in districts of Manhattan, however, ranged in value between $2.74 and $16 per square foot. In general, the Commission attributed to congestion a variety of physical and social evils similar to those emphasized by housing reformers for many years.

The Commission presented a series of

fourteen recommendations designed to reduce existing congestion and discourage future overcrowding. The most important of these included restrictions upon the height and lot coverage of buildings; measures to encourage a more efficient distribution of industry; a reduction of taxation upon buildings in order to discourage the holding of land for speculative purposes; extension of the rapid transit system to facilitate suburban migration; promotion of farm schools and garden training to help people adopt agriculture as a profession; a campaign by the Bureau of Industries and Immigration of the State Department of Labor to "encourage the immigrants to become farm laborers and to discourage the segregating of immigrants in congested sections of the city." These recommendations illustrate the intense interest of the Progressive municipal reformer in urban decentralization and, particularly, his desire to deflect immigrants from the congested industrial cities. For all practical purposes, however, nothing resulted from the Commission's labors. Its report was significant mainly as a symptom of the fact that municipal reformers and officials viewed congestion as a problem so unique and urgent that it merited the appointment of a special government commission of inquiry.

Perhaps the outstanding accomplishment of the New York CCP was in the field of city planning. In connection with a city planning exhibit held in Washington, D. C., in 1909, the CCP sponsored a conference with the intention of establishing a national planning association. Held in the spring of 1909 this meeting resulted in the creation of a National Conference on City Planning. On the national level the conference became a significant link between the housing and planning movements. Lawrence Veiller, for example, served on its executive committee and contributed numerous papers at the annual meetings. Planners, likewise, often participated in the sessions of the National Housing Association. Thus, after 1910, both the housing and planning movements had achieved national organization and shared a common interest in problems relating to housing, congestion, and urban decentralization.

The New York CCP, with similar interests, urged both planners and housing reformers to adopt its own special formula for the improvement of housing conditions and the relief of congestion. It stressed a program of land and taxation reform identified particularly with Benjamin C. Marsh. Though Marsh was not a doctrinaire single-taxer, he borrowed heavily from the theories of Henry George and his disciples.

The high cost of land, the CCP argued, was "an essential, eternal and irremediable cause of congestion of population so far as housing conditions are concerned. With expensive land no remedy for congestion among unskilled workers can permanently be found." Well-versed in European land and tax programs, Marsh saw in them clues to the radical improvement of housing conditions and congestion relief. Speaking of Frankfurt, Marsh noted that it had "pursued a consistent policy of land purchase and owned in 1907 about 48.9 [per cent] of the land within the city limits, and a large percentage outside the city limits." Other German cities owned large parcels of land. In the opinion of the CCP the American city might wisely emulate their example, acquiring land "for its purposes early — before speculation increases its cost." Municipal land ownership, the Committee argued, had numerous advantages. The city possessed a greater measure of control over the character and pace of its expansion, while it was assured a cheap supply of land for public improvements. Municipal land, if rented out or sold to limited-dividend companies, would encourage the production of better housing at lower costs. Tenements or homes erected upon land acquired at agricultural prices would be much cheaper than dwellings erected upon private land which had undergone the process of speculative transfer and subdivision.

As important as municipal land ownership, in the view of Marsh and the CCP, was the differential or graded tax. This involved a progressive tax upon increases in land values, of which the community received one-tenth to one-quarter, as well as the proceeds from the regular land tax. The differential tax, which taxed land at a much higher rate than buildings (thus transferring at least part of the "unearned increment" to the community) was clearly designed to discourage land speculation or monopoly and, conversely, to encourage improvements. Landowners, presumably, would find it too costly to keep land idle, waiting for it to increase in value. Large amounts of unimproved land would be thrown onto the market, depreciating the value of all land and promoting construction of homes and public improvements. Land, not improvements, bore the brunt of taxation.

Marsh envisioned vast benefits to the working class and city as a whole from the differential tax, at the expense only of the landholder and speculator. Cheaper land, in the first place, promised to reduce building costs and thus rents. Rents would drop also because landowners would have to pay the taxes currently assessed upon owners of improved property. Marsh thought the differential tax would take a "heavy burden" off industry, permitting the payment of higher wages and encouraging the "appropriate"

use of land. Finally, it would provide sufficient revenue to meet the "social needs" of the city.

The differential taxer like Marsh and the uncompromising single-taxer like Frederic C. Howe of Cleveland clearly regarded a program of restrictive legislation as a superficial response to the urban housing problem. From the point of view of tax reformers, any plan for "constructive" housing legislation was equally futile if it failed to control land values. "While poverty is explained by immigration," Howe argued, "by improvident marriages, by the Malthusian law of population, by the drink evil . . . the real cause is nearer at hand. It is to be found in the burden of rent, which is slowly, but none the less finally, appropriating the surplus wealth of the people." The speculator, Howe continued, throttled and strangled the development of the city. He withdrew a large percentage of every city's total land area from circulation to create scarcity, and thus appreciate values. As rents increased on remaining improved land, private dwellings gave way to apartment houses, and homes to slums.

The tax reformer hoped to accomplish directly what the exponent of the garden city anticipated indirectly — the reduction of congestion, the depreciation of land values, the lessening of rents, more and better housing. However, few American cities adopted a differential tax, and only two large ones — Seattle and Pittsburgh. The Pittsburgh law of 1913 reduced the tax on land compared to buildings by 10 per cent for 1914 and 1915, and continued the 10 per cent reductions every third year until the tax on buildings equalled half that on land. Despite the fond hopes of Marsh and Howe, radical tax reform had limited success. As we have seen, no garden city such as Letchworth appeared, no garden villages of the charm and beauty of Port Sunlight and Bournville; though some progress in good industrial housing had been made, there were few garden suburbs. The garden city ideal, especially where it involved cooperative landholding, presumed a degree of planning, of economic and social cooperation, and a predilection for wholesale community planning for which the average middle-class American was unprepared. The job- and wages-oriented labor movement represented by the AF of L had little inclination to indulge in cooperative housing experiments, let alone schemes of urban reconstruction. The reformer thus lacked a wide base of support for his community planning ideals. He had to depend upon a few benevolent businessmen or philanthropic agencies to promote his model communities. Similarly, few Americans would endorse experiments in municipal land ownership on a scale sufficient to affect radically the cost of land and character of urban expansion.

Yet the intensive concern of housing reformers, city planners, and the CCP in controlled urban growth finally paid a handsome dividend. Both the Boston tenement house law of 1899 and Veiller's Tenement House Law of 1901 restricted building heights to a certain multiple of street widths, and Los Angeles in 1909 had established use districts, prohibiting industry in a certain section of the city. In 1916 New York City adopted America's first comprehensive zoning code, enacted through the combined pressure of housing, taxation, and other social reformers in alliance with conservative business interests. Indeed, one small but powerful segment of New York's business community triggered the events which resulted in New York's

pioneering zoning measure. The reformer was not isolated in his zoning campaign, for businessmen possessed a direct, tangible economic stake in zoning which they lacked in the more visionary garden city ideal.

*   *   *

The New York zoning law of 1916, in which the interest of the social reformer like Veiller or Purdy in promoting the general welfare coincided with that of the businessman in protecting his investment, ranks with the New York Tenement House Law of 1901 as among the most significant municipal reforms of the Progressive era. By today's standards, certainly, the zoning resolution was inadequate. In striving to win unanimous support and to insure that the restrictions would not discourage real estate investment, the zoning commissions proved overgenerous to developers. The 1916 measure with subsequent amendments permitted New York City a potential resident population of more than 55 million. Just as Veiller had discouraged literal adoption of New York's housing laws, George B. Ford in 1916 warned other cities against slavish imitation of New York's zoning measure: "It would be most unfortunate if the law were applied as it stands to other cities for it is full of unduly liberal provisions in the way of height and size that tend strongly to defeat the object of the law but were necessitated by the exceptional economic conditions of New York."

The zoning legislation possessed a flaw, besides its liberality, which was not apparent to the housing reformers and planners of the early twentieth century. The zoning resolution of 1916 was a pioneering effort which aroused national interest and resulted in acceptance of zoning by hundreds of American communities in the following decade, but, like restrictive housing legislation, it was primarily negative in effect. Restrictive legislation and zoning provided municipalities with indispensable tools of control over physical development, and in this sense Progressive housing reform and planning marks an important transitional era; the problem, however, was that such negative legislation in itself represented a dead end. It could not clear slums, nor provide adequate housing for those elements of the population whom the commercial builder could not profitably accommodate, nor establish criteria for satisfactory residential environments. The planner of the period was at heart a social reformer anxious to improve housing conditions, but he thwarted his own purpose by embracing a negative zoning program and a wistful garden city rhetoric, thus surrendering any hopes of dealing with housing directly. The response of the first generation of American planners to the urban housing problem was deconcentration attained through zoning and the garden city and its variations, a strikingly indirect approach which proved ultimately ineffectual. It left the slums standing, and although it pointed to the need for relating housing and planning, it provided no concrete, workable basis for the coordination of housing and planning policy.

George E. Mowry: THE URBAN REFORM TRADITION

No historian has done as much as George E. Mowry to dispel the notion that the twentieth-century reform movements received their major impetus from the Populist movement. In this chapter from his book, The Era of Theodore Roosevelt, 1900–1912, *George E. Mowry stresses the indigenous character of urban reform movements in the late nineteenth and early twentieth centuries. He argues that "the role of the city as the inspirer of social democracy and as the originator of social regulation has been relatively overlooked in American history."*

THE large city in the United States by the opening of the century had gained an unenviable reputation as the natural home of political corruption, crime, and vice. There was certainly much evidence to support Lord Bryce's often-quoted remark that it was one of the worst-governed units in the democratic world. From the Atlantic coast to the Middle West and on to the Pacific the city appeared to be the favorite haunt of the venal, where regularly "offense's gilded hand shoved by justice and the wicked prize itself bought out the law." In New York, Jersey City, Chicago, St. Louis, and Minneapolis, and in San Francisco and Los Angeles, the tale read much the same: city councils for sale and mayors protecting criminals; water, gas, and street-railway franchises granted for fifty years or more to private corporations with the legal right to charge exorbitant

Pages 59–68 from *The Era of Theodore Roosevelt, 1900–1912,* by George E. Mowry. Copyright © 1958 by George E. Mowry. Reprinted by permission of Harper & Row, Publishers.

fees; police whose salaries were regularly enhanced by contributions from houses of prostitution and other noxious institutions; and politicians with such names as "Bath Tub" John Coughlin and "Hinky Dink" Kenna who methodically supplied the requisite votes on election day to keep the system operating. Meanwhile the ultimate victim of the graft, extortion, and jobbery saw his taxes mount, his water often contaminated, his sewage system fouled, his streetcars scheduled fortuitously, and his city adorned with ugly and ill-paved streets leading to noisome tenements.

Many descendants from the older stocks were quick to indict the new immigration for the unseemly conditions; but St. Louis with its long-settled Germanic population, Minneapolis with its Scandinavian tradition, and that transplanted Midwestern heaven, Los Angeles, approached, if they did not equal, the normative corruption of the East. Obviously, the true explanation for urban misgovernment was much more complex. A part of the reason for the condition lay in the speed with which American cities grew. This rate of growth, perhaps then unmatched in the world, placed enormous pressures on city governments for the rapid creation and extension of a multitude of new services. The new utility, street, and transportation contracts, all political and many monopolistic by nature, offered great rewards for successful bidders. And just at the time when the demands on city government were the greatest, the peculiar and fragmented character of the cities' new population, largely recruited from the American countryside and from southern and eastern Europe, made efficient urban government impossible. Large-city life almost demanded a collectivist and planning point of view, but the rural Ameri-

cans coming to the city were committed by tradition to a philosophy of individualism and private enterprise. The immigrants from southern and eastern Europe, desperately poor, often illiterate, and without a democratic heritage, were easy prey for the self-seeking boss. With added tensions centering around labor, racial, and religious questions, the result was chaos and corruption.

Even if the city had had a cohesive, intelligent, and interested citizenry devoted to the principle of urban planning, the path to efficient and honest government before 1900 would have been difficult. For few cities then had the power to grant franchises; in most instances that lay with the state governments. And in many commonwealths the ethics surrounding the statehouses were little better than those in the city chambers. Before the municipality could reform itself, it first had to cut the corrupt cord which led directly to the state capitals.

The multitudinous and pressing problems confronting the large city well before 1900 had not escaped critical citizens. Since the Tweed days Tammany Hall and its nefarious actions had excited sporadic and ill-sustained reform movements. Crime, vice, housing conditions, child labor, and the more prosaic subjects of sewage, transportation, and lighting facilities had all inspired citizens' investigating committees. But until the nineties little had been accomplished either in New York or in the rest of the country. What reform movements arose remained local in character and short-lived in time.

The defects in municipal life and government, however, became a subject of national discussion in the nineties. Within the five years after its founding in 1895, The *American Journal of Sociology* carried some thirteen scholarly articles dealing in a critical fashion with some phase of urban life. During the same period numerous questioning articles made their appearance in the more popular magazines. Dr. Albert Shaw's studies of English city governments in his *Review of Reviews* were objective and influential; a series by James D. Phelan in the *Arena* carried concrete suggestions for reformation by the practicing reform mayor of San Francisco. Phelan's demands for public ownership of municipal utilities, home rule, and provisions for direct legislation were elaborated in 1899 by Frank Parsons in his clinical and muckraking volume, *The City for the People.* A year later Gustavus Myers wrote *A History of Public Franchises in New York City* and followed it with *The History of Tammany Hall.*

Meanwhile in dozens of the nation's major cities small groups of reformers had already come together, usually in nonpartisan organizations, to discuss possible cures for the ills of city life. Such a group in Chicago coalesced around the leadership of Charles R. Crane, Walter L. Fisher, Victor F. Lawson, and William Kent. Another such group was formed by Dr. John Randolph Haynes of Los Angeles to further the move for direct legislation. Haynes's organization soon became state-wide and elicited the support of such California reformers as James D. Phelan, Rudolph Spreckels, and President Jordan of Stanford University. In 1894 the National Municipal League was organized, and by the end of the century Municipal Ownership Leagues, City Clubs, and Direct Legislation Leagues spotted the land. All were nonpartisan; all were reform-minded.

The accomplishments of these municipal reform organizations were not negligible. At a time when Bryan and his grass-rooted agrarian disciples were leading the national reform movement to defeat under the Democratic banner, these nonpartisan organizations were conducting a national campaign of education in street-corner politics. Here and there across the land they even succeeded in doing more than indoctrinating. After four unsuccessful attempts, San Francisco achieved a new city charter in 1893, which permitted home rule, public ownership, and the establishment of a city civil service. The charter also strictly limited the conditions under which franchises were to be granted to utility companies.

Simultaneously other cities were putting pressure on their state legislatures for similar grants of freedom. By 1900 the movement was well under way, and by the opening of the First World War twelve states, ten of which were west of the Mississippi River, had passed general home-rule legislation. Once freed of the legislative incubus, municipalities began to experiment broadly with their governments. Within a decade Galveston, Texas, had adopted the commission form of government, and Staunton, Virginia, had pioneered the city-manager type. By 1910 over a hundred major cities were using either the commission or the manager type of government.

During the quarter century after the Civil War the role of successful reform mayors is a short one. Grover Cleveland's career in Buffalo comes to mind, but few others. But beginning in 1889 a succession of colorful municipal leaders gained a national reputation for their work in urban politics. Hazen S. Pingree served four terms as mayor of Detroit before a grateful citizenry elected him governor of Michigan in 1896. A rich manufacturer, he gained a reputation during the depression days of the early nineties as a friend of the working class and as an opponent of business domination of civic utilities and politics. His personal war against long-term franchises and extortionate street-railway rates, and his "potato patch" plan for the unemployed, won national attention. Even more colorful was the career of a Toledo, Ohio, manufacturer, Samuel M. ("Golden Rule") Jones. A Welsh immigrant whose career began in the Pennsylvania oil fields, Jones gained a local reputation in Toledo for his labor policy. In his small but successful oil-equipment factory, he instituted profit sharing, the eight-hour day, a minimum wage, and paid vacations, and abolished the time-keeping system by permitting each workingman to keep his own time. An ethical anarchist, Jones fervently believed in the fundamental goodness of the human being, and deplored the crime of man's seeking power over other men. "I don't want to rule anybody," he remarked. "Each individual must rule himself."

Jones soon gained a national reputation when he was elected mayor as a fusion candidate of the Republicans and a local reform group, in 1897, only to repudiate the Republican machine that had supported him a short time before. Trouble developed when Jones refused to make the political payments expected by the regular politicians. What was worse, he insisted on infusing city government with his golden rule philosophy. One of his first deeds was to establish an open-air church where men of all faiths, including Jews and Catholics, preached and worshipped. Thereafter he took clubs away from the city police; established a free lodginghouse for tramps, free kindergartens, playgrounds, and night schools; constructed a municipal golf course; and set a minimum wage of $1.50 a day for municipal common labor when the prevailing wage was one dollar or less. Since every citizen of Toledo was a "member

of the family," no man had the right, he declared, to enslave another by political or economic bonds. Jones soon came to believe that "of all forms of capital" public ownership was the only economic system consistent with Christian ethics, whose political expression was democracy. "Private ownership," he remarked, "is a high crime against democracy." Jones was quickly deserted by the regular politicians and their machines. In 1903 both major parties campaigned against him, and the three Toledo newspapers even refused to print his letter accepting the nomination by a group of independents. Nevertheless, he ran four times, won four times, died in office, and was succeeded by his disciple, Brand Whitlock.

The same year that Toledo first elected "Golden Rule" Jones, San Francisco elected James D. Phelan mayor of San Francisco. Phelan, a wealthy banker, had been an anti-Bryan Democrat in 1896 at the same time he was allied with Rudolph Spreckels of the wealthy sugar family and the San Francisco Merchants' Association in a demand for the public ownership of the city's streetcar, telephone, water, gas, and electric services. During two years of effort San Francisco obtained a reform charter. But Phelan's administration and the businessmen's reform movement was abruptly ended by the famous strike of January, 1901, which resulted in the Union Labor party's victory of the following fall.

The reform spirit seemed to be moving rapidly in American cities in 1901. Seth Low, wealthy merchant, university president, and philanthropist, was elected mayor of New York with the avowed purpose of divorcing municipal affairs from national politics. In Cleveland, Ohio, a millionaire streetcar magnate and former congressman, Thomas Lofton Johnson, was victorious on a program of public ownership. Mark M. Fagan, like Johnson a disciple of Henry George, won in Jersey City. And in St. Louis a young public attorney, Joseph W. Folk, was prosecuting election frauds committed by the machine that had supported him. Johnson had a particularly interesting career. Starting as an impoverished Southerner, he had accumulated a fortune in city street railways and in steel. According to his own testimony, he was converted to free trade and the single tax by reading Henry George's *Progress and Poverty*. After serving two terms in Congress in the nineties, Johnson was elected mayor of Cleveland in 1901, a position which he held until defeated in 1909. A Jeffersonian Democrat, Johnson invariably demanded in his campaigns home rule, equal taxation, and municipal ownership or the "three-cent fare." But probably his greatest contribution to municipal life was his eight-year campaign for the political education of the citizens of Cleveland. He attracted a remarkable group of educated and liberal-minded young men around him as subordinate administrators, and at the end of his political career he left Cleveland, according to Lincoln Steffens, "the best governed city in America."

In 1902, the October issue of *McClure's Magazine* carried Lincoln Steffens' article "Tweed Days in St. Louis," which is usually cited as the start of muckraking, and which is often given credit for initiating a great wave of civic reform. The muckrakers obviously did not start the movement; it was well under way before their first articles appeared. It is probably more accurate to say that the reform spirit created the muckrakers and the muckrake magazines. Before 1890 the periodical field had been dominated by the traditional high-priced quality magazines, which devoted much of their space to literature, the arts, and polite fiction. After that date the rising curve of literacy and technical advance resulting in cheaper paper and printing first made possible real mass circulation. A number of periodicals selling for as little as ten cents appeared, but until 1902 their subject matter differed little save in quality from the older publications. After the appearance of Lincoln Steffens' article in the September *McClure's* describing the corruption of the St. Louis government and another by Ida Tarbell the following month, originating a popular and sharply critical history of the Standard Oil Company, a revolution occurred in the periodical press. When *McClure's* sales soared skyward, *Munsey's, Cosmopolitan, Everybody's, Hampton's, Pearson's, Success*, and even some of the more elite publications sought to copy the same formulas. As the American appetite for the new literature appeared to be insatiable, a large group of the nation's first-rate periodical writers were attracted to the movement. In addition to Lincoln Steffens and Ida Tarbell, Upton Sinclair, Mark Sullivan, Ray Stannard Baker, David Graham Phillips, Charles E. Russell, Samuel Hopkins Adams, and a host of lesser talents joined the campaign of exposure. Collectively their articles pried into practically every political, economic, and moral problem of the age. They attacked the evils of city, state, and national government, labor unions, big business, Wall Street, life insurance, the press, the medical profession, the food industry, child labor, women's inequality, prostitution, and the drug trade. Heavily factual in content, critical in tone, and full of righteous but optimistic indignation, the average muckrake article presented no curative proposals, but simply sought to give the average citizen a scientific description of what was wrong with the varied sectors of American life. Taken as a whole, the impact of the muckrake literature was enormous. Before this journalistic crusade had run its course, few literate Americans could have any real feelings of complacency about their civilization. Steffens' painfully specific series of articles describing the wayward governmental operations of one major city after another, for example, was calculated to awaken even the most patriotic citizen to the evils in his home town. And a later series on urban reformers made him aware of what had been accomplished elsewhere. Within six years after Steffens' "Shame of the Cities" series had appeared, formidable reform movements had appeared in Philadelphia, Chicago, Kansas City, Minneapolis, Los Angeles, and San Francisco.

Meanwhile, some of America's major cities had become the centers of another sort of reform activity, which had been inspired abroad. After visiting English settlement houses, Jane Addams came back to her native Illinois to establish, in 1889, Chicago's Hull House. Around this institution in the slums gathered a remarkable group of women. Julia Lathrop, the first woman member of the Illinois Board of Charities, was there, as was Florence Kelley, the first factory inspector of the state. Miss Kelley later went on to New York to become associated with Lillian Wald at the Henry Street Settlement. This energetic group of women and their associates were to be largely responsible for changing and broadening the old concept of wardship into a new police power which permitted the states to protect women and children at home and at work.

The rising tendency to throw the protective arm of the state around women and children also influenced the develop-

ment of the juvenile court, which originated in an Illinois law of 1899 and soon spread across the country east to New York and west to Denver, where Judge Ben B. Lindsey became nationally known for his twenty-five-year effort to protect and reform wayward youth. Much of the same sentiment helped to inspire the New York Committee of Fifteen, organized in 1900 to investigate housing conditions in the "lower depths" of the city. The committee, which included among its members Jacob H. Schiff, John D. Rockefeller, Jr., and George Foster Peabody, soon extended its work into the associated areas of public health and prostitution. Its findings were partially responsible for the 1901 state building law, which included minimum standards for lighting, sanitation, and ventilation, and fire precautions.

The role of the city as the inspirer of social democracy and as the originator of social regulation has been relatively overlooked in American history. The "gas and water socialism" of American cities during the first decade of the twentieth century persuaded many nonsocialistic Americans to accept the principle of limited public ownership. In 1896 less than half of the waterworks were owned by municipalities. By 1915 almost two-thirds of them were owned and operated by city governments. Less but still significant progress was made in the field of gas, electricity, and public transportation. In the local elections of 1911 it is interesting to note that the Socialist party carried eighteen cities in the country and almost won ten or a dozen more, and this at a time when the Socialist vote in state-wide elections was all but negligible. The city also either passed or inspired the passage of the first significant labor, housing, and public health legislation. Although the Grangers were responsible for the introduction of the regulatory commission, it was the city that first used it so effectively, on such a scale, and in such an intimate fashion that its virtues were brought home to the masses of the people. To a larger degree than has been recognized, it was the city that both blazed the way and supplied the pressure for the passage of much of the state regulatory enactments in the new century.

In November, 1902, the Ohio legislature passed a new municipal code for cities with a population of over 5,000 people. The code took much of the appointive power away from mayors and placed it in the city council or in the governor of the state. It was obviously aimed at Ohio's radical mayors. Johnson and Jones found in Ohio what Mark Fagan and George Record found in Jersey City and what Joseph Folk encountered in St. Louis. Since the city was the servant of the state, urban control was not enough; to reform the city

one had to reform the statehouse and the governor's mansion. Pingree, Jones, Johnson, Folk, Phelan, Record, Kent, Spreckels, and Crane carried their movements to the state, either leading a reform crusade or supporting one. Even when their personal stars fell, they carried to the state a new street-corner political philosophy based upon such urban things as utility franchises, tenement houses and slums, public health, the social conditions of women and children, factory legislation, and the war in the streets between capital and labor. George Record's "New Idea" Republicans never did obtain a majority in New Jersey, but as their historian has said, "the remarkable Wilson legislation of 1911 would have been impossible without them." When this new middle-class, urban-minded reform strain was added to the older agrarian one, the existing political structure with its ideological and economic implications began to crumble.

Carl N. Degler: POLITICAL PARTIES AND THE RISE OF THE CITY

In this article, originally published in the Journal of American History, *Carl N. Degler convincingly demonstrates the prodigious effect of the city on the two major political parties beginning in the mid-1890's. "It was the political activity of the urban voters," he writes, "which raised the Republican party to a position of dominance ... for a third of the century, just as it has been the cities which have been largely responsible for the Democratic party's leading place ... for the most recent third of this century."*

THE ending of Reconstruction in 1877 deprived both Republican and Democratic parties of the issues that had sustained their rivalry for half a century. As a result, in the Presidential elections from 1876 to 1892, neither party won deci-

From Carl N. Degler, "American Political Parties and the Rise of the City: An Interpretation," *Journal of American History* (June, 1964), pp. 41–59. Reprinted by permission of the Organization of American Historians.

sively; never before nor since has popular political inertia been so noticeable. More important, this indecision of the voters obscured the significant fact that the Republican party was popularly weak. For despite the preponderance of Republican Presidents during these years, only James A. Garfield secured a popular plurality and his was the smallest in history. The party's weak popular base was even more evident in the congressional elections between 1874 and 1892 when the Democrats captured sizable majorities in the House of Representatives in eight out of ten Congresses. So serious was this popular weakness of the party that Republican Presidents from Rutherford B. Hayes to Benjamin Harrison, as both Vincent P. De Santis and Stanley P. Hirshson have shown, worked in a variety of ways to build up a stronger Republican party in the South, but with very limited success.

Thus in the opening years of the 1890's the Republicans as a national party were in obvious trouble. The elections of 1890 and 1892 were disastrous for them as the Democrats swept into firm control of the House of Representatives and into the White House as well. Despite the party's proud association with the winning of the War for the Union, the Republicans were no more popularly based than at their founding forty years earlier; the majority of the nation's voters remained stubbornly Democratic. Moreover, with each passing election the political value of that vaunted association depreciated further as memories grew dimmer. The party seemed destined to recapitulate the history of the Whigs by serving only as a convenient alternative to the Democrats.

At that point, though, a complete reversal in party prospects took place. In the congressional election of 1894 the Re-

publicans clearly emerged as the majority party, leaving the Democrats to wander in the political wilderness for a generation. The transfer of seats in the election of 1894 from the Democratic to the Republican side of the House was the largest in history. The Republicans gained a majority of 132, whereas in twenty-four states not a single Democrat was elected and in six others only one Democrat was returned in each. Moreover, prominent Democrats like William L. Wilson of West Virginia, William McK. Springer of Illinois, and Richard L. Bland of Missouri — men associated with important Democratic doctrines like low tariffs and free silver — lost their places. This overwhelming Republican congressional victory in 1894 was confirmed two years later by what for the Republicans was to be their first decisive Presidential victory without benefit of federal protection of Negro voting in the South. Measured against the margins of defeat in previous elections, William Jennings Bryan's defeat was crushing; he ran farther behind the winner than any candidate of a major party since Ulysses S. Grant trounced Horace Greeley.

Dramatic as the Republican victories for 1894 and 1896 undoubtedly were, their enduring significance lies in the continuance of the trend they began. For the next sixteen years the Republicans, without interruption, commanded the majorities in the House and elected the Presidents. Thus in the middle of the 1890's the Republicans, for the first time, emerged as the majority party of the nation.

The question which arises is: why? At the outset one can reject the hypothesis of challenging new leadership, since the party enjoyed none in the 1890's. Furthermore, since the shift in votes took place when Grover Cleveland, an acknowledged conservative, was President, and continued when a radical Democrat, Bryan, was the party's candidate, the policies of the opposition party do not offer much help in explaining the change. The only place left to look is among the voters themselves. It is their attitudes that changed as the United States passed from an agricultural to an industrial economy.

In spite of all that has been written to emphasize that the 1890's was the period during which this agrarian to industrial transition occurred, there are valid reasons for placing this momentous shift in the preceding decade. It was, for example, during the 1880's that the production of manufactured goods surpassed farm goods in dollar value, and it was in this same decade that a majority of the nation's work force became engaged in non-agricultural rather than agricultural pursuits. Also during the 1880's railroad construction reached unprecedented heights, with more miles of track laid than in any other decade in American history. These were years of peak membership of the Knights of Labor, something over 700,000; the American Federation of Labor was formed, and the number of industrial strikes sharply increased. It was the decade of the frightening Haymarket riot in Chicago, which, in its nationwide notoriety, epitomized the arrival of the new world of the factory, the city, and the immigrant. In fact the number of immigrants who flooded into the country in that decade exceeded that of any other similar period in the century. Furthermore, those ten years were the seedtime of the city. According to a contemporary analysis of the census, the number of cities with 8,000 or more population jumped from 286 in 1880 to 443 in 1890. Many cities doubled in size in the ten years, and some, like Chicago,

had been already large at the beginning of the decade. A few made spectacular records of rapid growth. Minneapolis jumped from 47,000 to 165,000; Omaha reached 140,000 in 1890, though ten years before its population had been no more than 31,000; Denver nearly tripled its population.

During that decade of transition neither the political parties nor the people were prepared by previous experience for the problems and nature of the new industrial, urban age. Hence the politics of the 1880's were sterile, uninteresting, and often trivial, as the parties and the voters rehashed stale issues and only reluctantly faced the new. Then, in the early 1890's, it would seem, the decision was made; the commitment of the voters hardened. The question then remains: why did the Republican party, which thus far had been sectionally based and numerically weak, rather than the popular Democratic party, emerge from this period of indecision as the dominant party of the nation?

A part of the answer seems to lie in the public image of the two parties. The Republican party was more suited to the needs and character of the new urban, industrial world that was beginning to dominate America. In those years the Republicans were the party of energy and change. They inherited from their antebellum beginnings as well as from the experience of Reconstruction a tradition which looked to the national authority first and to the states second. The party and its leaders had not hesitated to use the national power in behalf of economic growth by sponsoring such measures as the Homestead Act, land grants and loans to railroad construction companies, and protective tariffs. During the Civil War the Republicans demonstrated their willingness to use income and inheritance taxes, and fiat money when the nation's survival had seemed to require such novel measures. In the 1880's, it was Republican Senator Henry W. Blair who sought to employ the federal revenues and power in behalf of aid to the public schools. In each of the four times that the Blair education bill came before the Congress, Republican support always exceeded Democratic support.

This nationalistic tradition and these specific measures, of course, also added up to a national image of the party that would appeal to urban voters and immigrants. As the self-proclaimed party of prosperity and economic growth, the Republicans could expect to win support from those who manned the expanding factories and crowded into the tenements of the burgeoning cities. Certainly party spokesmen made appeals to the urban working class. In 1892, for example, President Harrison told the Congress:

I believe that the protective system, which has now for something more than thirty years continuously prevailed in our legislation, has been a mighty instrument for the development of our national wealth and a most powerful agency in protecting the homes of our workingmen from the invasion of want. I have felt a most solicitous interest to preserve to our working people rates of wages that would not only give daily bread, but supply a comfortable margin for those home attractions and family comforts and enjoyments without which life is neither hopeful nor sweet.

Nor should such appeals be hastily brushed aside as empty rhetoric. Republican claims received substance, if not proof, from the steady rise in real wages during the last three decades of the century. Moreover, foreign observers, like Friedrich Engels, who certainly could not be accused of being partial to Republican propaganda, cited the tariff as one of the principal reasons why American workingmen were better off than European. In 1893 Engels wrote to his friend Friedrich A. Sorge that "through the protective tariff system and the steadily growing domestic market the workers must have been exposed to a prosperity no trace of which has been seen here in Europe for years now. . . ."

The Democratic party, to a greater extent than the Republican party, was more a congeries of state organizations than a national party. Certainly in the South and in a northern state like Illinois, there were many Democrats in the 1890's who were far from agreement with the national leadership. But even with these cautionary observations, of the two parties between 1880 and 1896, the Democrats undoubtedly presented the more conservative face to the electorate. The hallmark of the party under the dominance of Cleveland was economy, which in practice meant the paring down of government assistance to business, opposing veterans' pensions, hoarding the national resources, lowering the tariff, and, in general, stemming the Republican efforts to spur economic growth and to enhance the national power. Besides, the Democrats were ideologically unsuited to any ventures in the expansion of governmental activities. Still steeped in the Jeffersonian conception of the limited role of the federal government, the national Democrats were less likely than the Republicans to use federal powers in new ways to meet new problems. It was Cleveland, after all, who had vetoed a meager $10,000 relief appropriation for drought-stricken Texas farmers with the stern warning: "though the people support the Government the Government should not support the people."

The election results of the 1880's suggest that the Republicans were even then receiving returns from their bid for working class support. Today it is axiomatic that the big cities of the country will vote Democratic, but in that period most of the large urban centers outside the South were more likely to be Republican than Democratic. It is true that cities like New York, Boston, and San Francisco were usually safely Democratic, but in the three Presidential elections of the 1880's a majority of the nation's cities over 50,000 outside the South went Republican. In these three elections — even though in two of them Cleveland polled a larger vote than his Republican opponents — eastern and midwestern cities like Philadelphia, Chicago, Cleveland, Cincinnati, Buffalo, Providence, Milwaukee, Newark, Syracuse, Paterson, and Minneapolis invariably appeared in the Republican column. In the election of 1884, which was won by Democrats, the Republicans captured twenty of the thirty-three non-southern cities over 50,000. In 1888 the Republicans took twenty-six of the forty-four largest non-southern cities listed in the census of 1890.

Furthermore, many of these Republican cities contained substantial proportions of immigrants. The 1890 census showed thirty percent or more of the population of Chicago, Milwaukee, Paterson, Cleveland, Buffalo, Pittsburgh, Providence, and Rochester to be foreign-born. All of these cities voted consistently Republican in the three Presidential elections of the 1880's.

But the tendency for Republicans to do better than Democrats in northern cities must not be exaggerated. The election of 1892, with its upsurge of Democratic strength in the cities, demonstrated that Republican popularity in the urban centers was neither so overwhelming nor so fixed that the popular Democracy might

not reduce it. Clearly some other force, some other ingredient in the mixture, was operative. That additional factor appears to be the depression of 1893.

The depression of the 1890's was an earth-shaker. Not only did it last five years or more, but it was the first economic decline since the United States had made the transition to full-scale industrialism. As a consequence its effects were felt especially in the growing cities and among the working class. A recent historian of this depression has estimated that real earnings for the population dropped eighteen percent between 1892 and 1894. The single year of 1894 witnessed Coxey's army as well as other less well-known armies of unemployed workers on the march, widespread labor unrest, and the violence of the Pullman and Chicago railroad strikes. More workers went out on strike in that year than in any other in the century. The number was not equalled again until 1902.

Since it is true that the Republicans for all their belief in the national power would not have taken any stronger anti-depression measures than the incumbent Democrats, the election upset of 1894 might be considered as nothing more than a case of blind, rather than calculated, reprisal against the incumbents. Furthermore, it might be said that the Republicans had been chastised in much the same fashion in 1874 when they chanced to be in power at the beginning of the depression of 1873. The objection is not as telling as it appears. In the election of 1894 there was a third party, and if simple dissent were operating, the Populists should have benefited as much from it as the Republicans. But this they did not do. Although the total Populist vote in 1894 was higher than in 1892, not a single state that year, John D. Hicks has observed, could any longer be called predominantly Populist. Four western states, Kansas, Colorado, North Dakota, and Idaho, all of which had voted Populist in 1892, went Republican in 1894. In a real sense, then, the election was a victory for the Republican party and not simply a defeat for the Democrats.

If the terrible impact of the depression polarized the voting in a new way, thereby helping to explain the massive shift to the Republicans, the activities of the Democrats in 1896 could only confirm the urban voters in their belief that the Republican party was the more responsive political instrument. In their convention of 1896 the Democrats hardly noticed the cities; they had ears only for the cries of the farmers demanding currency reform. Many Populists, it is true, stood for something more than free silver, but the money issue was certainly accepted by Bryan and the vast majority of Democrats as the principal issue of the campaign. Free silver was at best uninteresting to the urban population and, at worst, anathema to them. The adoption of such a monetary policy would be inflationary and therefore contrary to the interests of all urban consumers, whether bankers, petty clerks, or factory workers. Mark Hanna, McKinley's campaign manager, sensed this defect in Bryan's appeal from the outset. Early in the campaign he said about Bryan: "He's talking silver all the time, and that's where we've got him."

And they did have him. The cities, where the industrial workers were concentrated, voted overwhelmingly Republican. Only twelve of the eighty-two cities with a population of 45,000 or more went for Bryan — and seven of the twelve were in the Democratic South while two others were located in silver-producing states. Seven of the seventeen cities in the states that Bryan carried gave a majority to McKinley; on the other hand,

only three of the sixty-five cities in states going to McKinley provided a majority for Bryan. Bryan was hopeless in the industrial East; he did not carry a single county in all of New England, and only one in New York, and eleven rural counties in Pennsylvania. He even lost normally Democratic New York City.

Taken together, the elections of 1894 and 1896 mark the emergence of the Republican party as the party of the rising cities. Even a cataclysmic event like the Civil War, in which the Democrats were on the losing side, had not been able to dislodge the Democracy from its favored place in the voters' hearts. But the impact of an industrial-urban society with its new outlook and new electorate had done the trick. It is significant that several cities like San Francisco, Detroit, Indianapolis, Columbus, and St. Paul, which had been Democratic in the 1880's and early 1890's, voted Republican in 1896 and remained Republican well into the twentieth century. None of the large cities which had been Republican in the 1880's and early 1890's, on the other hand, changed party affiliation in 1896 or for decades thereafter. Another indication of the continuity between the elections of 1894 and 1896 is that the states which showed the greatest Republican congressional gains in 1894 also showed increased Republican strength in the Presidential election two years later. There were twelve states, each of which gave the Republicans four or more new seats in 1894; of these, eight were among the states which in 1896 showed the greatest number of new counties going to the Republicans. Significantly, they were mainly industrial-urban states like Illinois, New Jersey, New York, Ohio, and Pennsylvania.

It is commonplace for textbooks to depict the Republican party of the late nineteenth century as the political arm of the Standard Oil Trust, but if the election returns are to be given any weight at all, that is not the way the voters saw the party in the 1890's. Not only was it the party of respectability, wealth, and the Union; it was also the party of progress, prosperity, and national authority. As such it could and did enlist the support of industrial workers and immigrants as well as merchants and millionaires. As one analyst of the 1896 New England vote saw it, the Democrats may have obtained their most consistent support among the poor and the immigrants of the cities, but the Republicans gained strength there, too, "just as they did in the silk-stocking wards. . . . They were able to place the blame for unemployment upon the Democrats and to propagate successfully a doctrine that the Republican party was the party of prosperity and the 'full dinner pail.'"

Ideologically, it is true, the Republican party in the 1890's had a long way to travel before it would translate its conception of the national power into an instrument for social amelioration. But it is suggestive that Robert M. La Follette in Wisconsin and Theodore Roosevelt in Washington, who are the best known of the early Progressives, were also Republicans. It is these men, and others like them in the party, who carried on the political revolution of 1894, which had first announced the Republican party as the majority party in the new America of cities and factories.

The significance of that political revolution is that the pattern of party allegiance then established continued for many years to come. To be sure, in 1912, because of a split in the Republican party, Woodrow Wilson was able to break the succession of Republican Presidents. But it is also evident that the success of the Democrats in 1912 and 1916 should not be taken as a sign of a fundamental change in voter preferences. One reason for thinking so is that in 1916 Wilson was reelected by the very close margin of 600,000 popular and twenty-three electoral votes and in 1920 the Republicans swept back into the White House on a landslide. Another reason is provided by the Democratic losses in the House of Representatives after 1912. That year the Democrats achieved a margin of 160 seats over the Republicans, one of the largest in congressional history, but by the mid-term elections the difference between the parties was down to 35; by 1916 it was less than 10. In 1918 the Democrats lost control of the House.

The most persuasive evidence for believing that the Republicans continued to be the majority party of the nation, despite the interruption of the Wilson administrations, is the history of elections during the 1920's. In 1920 Warren G. Harding received over 61 percent of the votes cast, a proportion of the total not achieved since the advent of universal manhood suffrage and only equalled once thereafter. Although other Republican presidential victories in the 1920's did not reach the proportions of the Harding landslide, they were all substantial. Furthermore, at no time between 1920 and 1928 was the Republican margin of strength in the House of Representatives endangered; it never went below twenty seats. In fact, near the end of the decade, Republican strength in the House was reaching out for a new high; in 1928 it was one hundred seats greater than the Democratic proportion. In the Presidential election that year Herbert Hoover's majority over Alfred E. Smith was more than six million votes. In short, by the end of the 1920's the Republicans were as much the majority party of the nation as they had been in 1894 when the tide of history first turned in their favor.

Within four years, though, another political revolution had been consummated, this time returning the Democrats to the position of the majority party of the nation. In 1932 the Democrats elected their second President in forty-two years and captured the House of Representatives with a majority of unprecedented size, something like 190 seats. The true measure of the reversal of political patterns, though, did not come until 1934 and 1936. For with their overwhelming victories in those two elections, the Democrats showed that 1932 was not simply another 1912, when a large Democratic victory had been quickly eroded away in subsequent elections. Instead, in 1934 the Democrats reversed the patterns of the preceding fifty years; rather than losing seats in the House, as was customary in off-year elections, they actually added ten more to their swollen total. And then in 1936 they succeeded in reelecting Franklin D. Roosevelt by an overwhelming majority, with a proportion of votes that came very near topping Harding's landslide of 1920.

Because the Roosevelt revolution in politics coincided with the onset of the Great Depression, it is tempting to argue that it was economic adversity in 1932, much as it had been in 1894, which accounts for the shift in the voters' preferences. Certainly the impact of the depression had much to do with the long-range change; it undoubtedly accounts for the overwhelming character of the shift. But there is also much evidence to suggest that the shift which first became evident in 1932 was already in progress four years before. Beneath the surface of Hoover's victory the forces which would consummate the Roosevelt revolution were already in motion in 1928 in behalf of Alfred E. Smith.

The most obvious comment to be made about Smith's vote was its large size.

Smith's 15 million votes were 6.5 million more than John W. Davis had polled in 1924, when La Follette's Progressive candidacy had drawn away some Democratic votes, and 5 million more than James M. Cox and Roosevelt had been able to capture in 1920. With this enormous gain, if by nothing else, Smith showed himself to be the most popular Democratic candidate since Bryan in 1896.

But important as Smith's ability to attract votes may have been, his contribution to the turn to the Democrats lay in something more than mere numbers. After all, Hoover increased the Republican vote by some five million over Coolidge's total in 1924 and Harding's in 1920. What was significant was that Smith's unique combination of politically effective personal attributes was attracting a new class of voters to the Democratic party. Many years after the election, Hoover pointed out that in 1928 the candidates of both major parties had risen from small beginnings to become figures of national prominence. But if this was true of the origins of Smith and Hoover, by 1928 the two men were poles apart. Unlike Hoover, or any previous presidential candidate of either party, Smith was both of lower class social background and a native of a big city. As is well known, his life and his career in politics were closely associated with New York City and the Tammany political machine. It is true that his four terms as governor of New York showed him to be progressive in thought and action as well as honest and courageous, but his loyalty to Tammany was both well known and unshakeable. Furthermore, Smith was a Roman Catholic and, though he had no intention of making his religion a political issue, many Protestants did. In fact, in 1927, an article that gained national prominence challenged him to show that his religion would not interfere with his proper execution of the duties of President. Although Smith's parents were native New Yorkers, his religion, his mother's Irish background and his close association with Irish-dominated Tammany Hall stamped him as a spokesman for the urban immigrants. In short, he was the first Presidential candidate to exhibit the traits of a part of the population that had never before been represented by a candidate of a major party.

Smith's religion, which hurt him in the South and helped to explain why Hoover was able to capture four southern states, undoubtedly assisted him in the North. Massachusetts and Rhode Island, both heavily Catholic in population, went Democratic in 1928 for the first time since the Civil War. In fact, while Hoover was taking 200 southern counties from the Democrats, Smith took 122 northern counties that had been consistently Republican. Moreover, of these 122 counties, 77 were predominantly Roman Catholic; most of these 77 counties remained in the Democratic column, it is worth emphasizing, in subsequent elections.

Since Roman Catholicism in America is an immigrant religion and its communicants are largely concentrated in the big cities, most of the new counties Smith gained were urban. Indeed, the striking thing about Smith's candidacy was that it attracted the big city vote away from the Republicans for the first time since the 1890's. In 1920 Harding had taken all of the twelve cities with a population over 500,000, but in 1928, among these twelve, New York, Cleveland, St. Louis, Milwaukee, and San Francisco went for Smith though their states did not. Moreover, Pittsburgh and Baltimore failed to give Smith a majority by fewer than 10,000 votes each. Of the twelve cities only Los Angeles was strongly for Hoover. If the votes of all twelve cities are added

together, Smith secured 38,000 more votes than Hoover; in 1920 the Republicans had carried the same cities by 1,638,000 votes. In a broader sample, a recent student of the election has shown that in 1920 Harding carried all twenty-seven of the principal cities outside the South; in 1928, Smith captured eight, and made appreciable gains in the others. He ran behind Cox and Roosevelt in only three of the twenty-seven. Such a reversal was one sign that a socio-political revolution was under way.

Despite all that has been written about Smith's appeal to the voters of the big cities, the significant point, often overlooked, is that his appeal was not of equal force in all cities. For example, he ran badly in southern cities, the residents of which exhibited, when compared with other southerners, the weakest commitment to the historic party principles that had made the South a stronghold of the Democrats. In fact, Dallas and Houston in Texas, and Birmingham in Alabama went Republican in 1928. More important was Smith's strikingly uneven attraction for the cities of the North. His attractive power was considerably stronger in those cities in which immigrant stock predominated than in those in which it was in the minority. (Immigrant stock is defined here as foreign-born whites and native whites born of one or more foreign-born parents.) According to the census of 1930, the closest to the election of 1928, there were thirty-six cities with populations in excess of a quarter of a million. In nineteen of these cities, immigrants and children of immigrants constituted 50 percent or more of the population. In the Presidential election of 1920, all of these nineteen cities voted Republican; in the election of 1924 all but one voted Republican. In the election of 1928, though, seven of them turned Democratic.

On the other hand, in the seventeen cities out of the thirty-six in which the native-born whites of native-born white parents constituted a majority of the population in 1930, only four went Democratic in 1928, and three of them were located in the traditionally Democratic South (Atlanta, New Orleans, and Memphis). The fourth was St. Louis. In fact, Democratic strength in these "native-white" cities actually declined in 1928, for in the 1920 and 1924 elections six of the seventeen had gone Democratic. All six of them, it should be noted, were in the Democratic South. Thus in the election of 1928 among the cities in which native whites constituted a majority, there was actually a loss in Democratic strength. In short, Smith's appeal to urban voters was not simply that he was of urban origin but that his Catholicism and Irish background stamped him as a champion of immigrants and children of immigrants. At the same time, those cities in which the immigrant stock was in the minority retained their allegiance to the Republican party — an allegiance which had been first clearly established in the 1890's for the big cities as a whole.

Yet it might be said that Smith failed, after all, to carry even a majority of the cities with a preponderance of immigrant stock. He won only seven of the nineteen cities of immigrant stock. Does not this fact call into serious question the assertion that there was a relationship between the social character of these cities and Democratic voting?

Closer analysis suggests not. As inspection of Table I makes evident, in every one of the cities with 50 percent or more immigrant stock, whether they were carried by Smith or not, the Democratic vote increased enormously in 1928 over 1920, when the Republican majorities had been very large. In fact, in none of the cities in which immigrant stock predominated was the Democratic increase less than 100 percent, and in many it was considerably higher. In these same cities, on the other hand, the Republican vote increased as much as 100 percent in only one of the nineteen cities and in only three did it go above 50 percent (Oakland, Pittsburgh, and Seattle). In several of the cities that Smith carried, the Republican vote actually fell from that of 1920.

If one examines the Democratic performance in those cities in which the native-white population predominated, the conclusion that there was a close association between the increase in Democratic votes and immigrant stock is further strengthened. In none of these cities was there much of an increase in either the total vote or in the vote for the Democratic candidate. (See Table II.) Only in Denver did the Democratic vote increase as much as 75 percent; in no city did it reach as high as 100 percent as it did in every one of the cities in Table I. In five the increase was less than 25 percent and in three there was actually a loss of Democratic votes. The median value is 26.0 percent.

The Republican vote in Table II provides a revealing contrast with the Democratic vote in Table I, for now it can be seen that the "native-white" cities produced no upsurge in voting for Republicans comparable to that in the cities of immigrant stock. Except for a marked — and what turned out to be temporary — upturn in Republican strength in the southern cities of Atlanta, Birmingham, Dallas, and Houston, the increase between 1920 and 1928 in none of these cities was as much as 100 percent. The median value is 53.2 percent.

From this examination of the variability in the response of the cities to Smith's candidacy it seems clear that Smith brought out the immigrant vote in

TABLE I
CITIES WITH FIFTY PERCENT OR MORE IMMIGRANT STOCK*

City	Democratic Vote in nearest thousand		Percent Change	Republican Vote in nearest thousand		Percent Change
	1920	1928		1920	1928	
Boston	68	205	202	108	99	−7.7
Buffalo	40	126	215	100	145	45.0
Chicago	197	716	266	635	812	27.8
Cleveland	71	166	132	149	195	30.7
Detroit	52	157	201	221	265	19.9
Jersey City	63	153	143	102	100	−1.9
Los Angeles	56	210	275	178	514	189.0
Milwaukee	25	111	344	73	82	12.2
Minneapolis	143	396	178	519	561	8.1
Newark	41	118	188	116	169	45.6
New York	345	1,168	239	786	715	−9.1
Oakland	21	61	190	73	119	63.2
Philadelphia	90	276	209	308	420	36.5
Pittsburgh	40	161	301	139	216	55.5
Providence	46	97	112	80	86	7.5
Rochester	29	74	156	74	100	35.2
St. Paul	21	57	171	40	53	32.5
San Francisco	33	97	195	96	96	0.0
Seattle	17	47	176	59	96	62.9

* Two cities in this list, Oakland and Seattle, counted 47.8 and 48.2 percent respectively of immigrant stock, but they have been included here rather than in Table II, because they also have less than 50 percent of native white population. Their proportions of native white population are 46.4 and 47.7 percent respectively. The missing proportions are accounted for by colored persons.

unprecedented numbers. Some of these voters of immigrant stock had probably been voting Republican all along and now switched to the Democrats. But many more, it would seem, voted for the first time, for otherwise one cannot explain the enormous increase in Democratic votes in the short span of eight years without a commensurate decline in Republican votes. These same people, backed by even greater numbers, would come out in 1932 to vote for Franklin Roosevelt and consummate the Roosevelt Revolution in politics. But it was Smith, the Catholic and the recognized champion of the urban-based immigrant, who first made the Democratic party the party of the cities and the immigrant. This up-

surge in immigrant voting in 1928 helps to explain, at least negatively, the apparent paradox of urban support for a Republican party in the 1920's that defended prohibition and pushed for restrictions on immigration. Prior to the galvanizing appearance of Smith on the political landscape, most urban immigrants just did not vote at all and many probably did not even think of themselves as part of the body politic. And to those who did vote, the Democratic party offered no candidates, other than Wilson, to lure them away from the party of national power, Theodore Roosevelt, and prosperity. Samuel Lubell has suggested, further, that the broadening educational opportunities of the 1920's also help to

TABLE II

CITIES WITH LESS THAN FIFTY PERCENT OF IMMIGRANT STOCK

Cities	Democratic Vote in nearest thousand		Percent Change	Republican Vote in nearest thousand		Percent Change
	1920	1928		1920	1928	
Akron	28	32	14.3	44	79	79.5
Atlanta	9	7	−22.5	3	6	100.0
Baltimore	87	126	44.8	126	135	7.3
Birmingham	25	17	−32.0	7	18	157.0
Cincinnati	78	110	41.0	113	148	31.0
Columbus	48	47	−2.3	60	92	53.2
Dallas	14	17	21.4	5	27	440.0
Denver	23	41	78.5	44	74	68.1
Houston	15	22	47.7	8	27	237.0
Indianapolis	61	73	19.7	80	110	37.4
Kansas City, Mo.	77	97	26.0	80	127	58.6
Louisville	56	64	14.3	68	98	44.3
Memphis	16	18	12.5	9	12	33.3
New Orleans	33	56	70.0	18	14	−22.2
Portland, Ore.	28	45	60.5	45	76	68.8
St. Louis	106	176	66.0	163	162	−0.68
Toledo	30	45	50.0	52	78	50.0

explain the upsurge in immigrant political participation in 1928.

Despite familiarity with the connection between the cities and the Democratic party today, that connection was not forged, as far as the nation was concerned, until 1928–1932. Indeed it is the conclusion of this paper that it was the political activity of urban voters which raised the Republican party to a position of dominance in American politics for a third of a century, just as it has been the cities which have been largely responsible for the Democratic party's leading place in the nation's political life for the most recent third of this century. For Franklin Roosevelt after the landslide of 1936 continued to receive the support of the vast majority of the 37 principal cities of over 250,000 population, carrying 32 of them in 1940 and 30 in 1944. Harry Truman in 1948 did about as well, even though the Dixiecrat candidate took three of the traditionally Democratic southern cities. Truman's score was 30 of the big cities against 4 for Thomas E. Dewey.

The real test of the Democratic power in the cities came in 1952 with the first campaign of Dwight D. Eisenhower, certainly the most popular Republican of the twentieth century. In that election and the next, Eisenhower made substantial inroads into the urban territory of the Democrats. In his first election, for example, he carried 21 of the 39 cities over 250,000 and in 1956 he did even better by taking 28 of them — almost as many as Franklin Roosevelt did in 1944.

But there are two good reasons for seeing this resurgence of Republican strength in the cities as temporary and nothing more than a reflection of the special appeal of Eisenhower rather than as a basic shift in popular party allegiance. The first reason is that Eisenhower was able to carry a majority of the House of Representatives for his party in only the first of his four congressional elections. Indeed, his own popular vote in 1956 was greater than that of 1952, but he proved unable, nonetheless, to do what every popular President since Zachary Taylor had been able to do: carry a majority of his party into the House of Representatives.

In this failure the cities played a part since many of them that voted for Eisenhower did not grant the same degree of support to the Republican congressional candidates. This tendency was most obvious in the southern cities, where he showed great strength. In 1952 he carried six of the eight southern cities and in 1956 he captured all but Atlanta. Yet in the congressional races in all of these cities, Democratic congressmen, because of the South's one-party system, were almost invariably returned. More important, the same tendency could be observed in cities outside the South. For example, in the Ninth Ohio District (Toledo) a Democratic congressman was returned in all four of Eisenhower's congressional elections, though the General personally carried the city in 1952 and 1956. Although Eisenhower won Cook County, Illinois in 1956, eight of the twelve congressional districts of the city of Chicago went Democratic. Newark and Denver, both of which supported Eisenhower in 1952 and 1956, sent only Democratic congressmen to Washington throughout the Eisenhower years. Eisenhower won Milwaukee in 1956, but the two congressmen elected from the city that year were Democrats.

The second reason for seeing Eisenhower's substantial victory as more personal than partisan is that in the election of 1960 John F. Kennedy, despite his close victory in the national popular vote, regained the cities for the Democrats. He carried 27 of the 39 cities, even though he did less well than Stevenson in 1952 among southern cities, capturing only New Orleans, San Antonio, and everfaithful Atlanta. A large part of the explanation for Kennedy's failure to regain southern big city support commensurate with his general increase in urban backing is to be found, of course, in southern dislike of the Democratic party's stand on civil rights which began with Truman and which Kennedy went out of his way to support and advance. Nevertheless, the defection also calls attention to the quite different social character of southern, as compared with northern big cities. There are very few Catholics or children of immigrants in southern cities, so that an Al Smith and a John F. Kennedy have no religious or social appeal there as they do in the North. That this difference was influential is suggested by the return to the Democratic fold in 1960 of San Antonio and New Orleans, the only two southern cities containing substantial numbers of Catholics and children of immigrants.

In short, as the congressional strength of the Democrats throughout the Eisenhower years had suggested, the election of 1960 showed that the Democrats still retained the long-term allegiance of the big city voters, whose support had first been evident thirty-two years before in another campaign by a Roman Catholic grandson of an Irish immigrant.

Suggestions for Additional Reading

By far the best general account of the rise of the industrial city in the late nineteenth and early twentieth centuries can be found in Charles N. Glaab and A. Theodore Brown, *A History of Urban America* (New York, 1967). The most detailed account is Blake McKelvey, *The Urbanization of America, 1860–1915* (New Brunswick, N. J., 1963). Still quite valuable is Arthur M. Schlesinger, *The Rise of the City* (New York, 1933).

Attitudes toward the city are treated in Morton and Lucia White, *The Intellectual Versus the City* (Cambridge, Mass., 1962). Although the Whites concern themselves primarily with American intellectuals from Thomas Jefferson to Frank L. Wright, their book is useful to the period we are considering. Also helpful on this subject are the documents in David R. Weimer, ed., *City and Country in America* (New York, 1962).

Numerous books have been written on political corruption in cities. Lincoln Steffens, *The Shame of the Cities* (New York, 1904) is a classic, as is Lord Bryce, *American Commonwealth*, Vol. I (London, 1888). One of the best of the more recent works is Walton Bean, *Boss Ruef's San Francisco* (Berkeley, 1952). The one book which covers most of the famous Gilded Age bosses is Harold Zink, *City Bosses in the United States* (Durham, N. C., 1930). The two most recent books on Boss Tweed of New York are Seymour Mandelbaum, *Boss Tweed's New York* (New York, 1965), and Alexander Callow, Jr., *The Tweed Ring* (New York, 1966). There are many muckraking accounts of the political machines. The most famous is M. R. Werner, *Tammany Hall* (New York, 1928).

In recent years countless books and articles have appeared on reform in the late nineteenth and early twentieth centuries. A first-rate book on the muckrakers is Louis Filler, *Crusaders of American Liberalism* (New York, 1939). Arthur Mann, *Yankee Reformers in the Urban Age* (Cambridge, Mass., 1954) is an excellent study of the Gilded Age roots of Progressive era reform in Boston. Eric Goldman, *Rendezvous with Destiny* (New York, 1952), and Richard Hofstadter, *The Age of Reform: From Bryan to F.D.R.* (New York, 1955), presenting conflicting interpretations of the reform movement, are both indispensable. Any student interested in urban poverty, and the attempts to provide solutions to this problem, must read Robert Bremner, *From the Depths: The Discovery of Poverty in the United States* (New York, 1956).

Historians are beginning to pay attention to individual cities in the period between 1865 and World War I, yet there is much that remains to be written. One of the best works to appear to date is Stephen Thernstrom, *Poverty and Progress: Social Mobility in a Nineteenth Century City* (Cambridge, Mass., 1964). Sam Warner, *Streetcar Suburbs: Process of Growth in Boston, 1870–1900* (Cambridge, Mass., 1963) is an extremely refreshing approach to local history. An interesting account of Progressivism in a southern city is William Miller, *Memphis During the Progressive Era, 1900–1917* (Madison, Wis., 1957). There are several urban biographies that cover the period extremely well. Bayrd Still, *Milwaukee* (Madison, Wis., 1945) is good. The period is treated well by Blake McKelvey, *Rochester*, Vols. II and III (Cambridge, Mass., 1949, 1956), and by Constance M.

Green, *Washington: Capital City, 1879–1950* (Princeton, N. J., 1963).

Students who wish to probe further into American urban history should look at the bibliographical essays by Allen F. Davis, "The American Historian versus the City," *Social Studies*, LVI, Part I (March, 1965), pp. 91–96; Part II (April, 1965), pp. 127–135; and Charles N. Glaab, "The Historian and the American City: A Bibliographic Survey," in Philip Hauser and Leo Schnore, eds., *The Study of Urbanization* (New York, 1965).

1 2 3 4 5 6 7 8 9 0